Tiptoe Through Genesis

Nancy Reuben Greenfield

Delightfully
DIFFERENT
publishing

Tiptoe Through Genesis

ISBN: 978-0-98581618-6

Second Edition

Published in the United States of America by Delightfully Different Publishing Dallas, TX

Cover Art and Book Design: Denise Houseberg

Special thanks to: Susan Herzfeld and Yosef Greenfield for their input.

Printed in the United States of America

NOTE: Please be respectful and refrain from taking into bathroom.

Table of Contents

Acknowledgements

Thank you
God
my children
family, friends and community

all my teachers

and especially
my husband Richard.

Thank you
for all your love and support.

It continues
to mean the world to me.

Nancy's Note

The Five Books of Moses
Genesis, Exodus, Numbers, Leviticus, Deuteronomy
are known as the written Torah.

This first book of

בראשית

is transliterated as **Bereshit**
and translated into Greek as **Genesis.**

There is
a.necessary fence
around the Torah
to preserve its purity.

The purpose of my book
is to create
a respectful bridge across this fence
so the original text
can easily be accessed
by people of all backgrounds.

Adaptation Goals

#1 Keeping it short.

This format allows you to read it through in
one sitting, over time, daily, weekly
when you need help, hope or
whenever the mood strikes.

#2 Keeping it easy.

Since biblical names, relationships
and time lapses can be very confusing
text has been added in brackets for clarification
or to introduce passages.
{example of added text in brackets}

#3 Keeping it flowing.

To keep things moving, this book
leaves out, condenses or alludes to
lists of details
like lineage and wars and journeys.

#4 Keeping the poetry.

Relying on a variety of English
translations and sources
each word was chosen for its accuracy
and poetic power.

#5 Keeping it verifiable.

Every Torah translation is
unique in its word choices so it
would be very rare for my
adapted text
to match word for word with your translation.

To compare any passage
use traditional biblical notation
(Portion, Section, Line) starting with Genesis 1:1.
For example: Portion Noah 9:8-17.
Go to the 9th Section and read Lines 8 through 17.
Note: Any bracketed {added text} is not included
in notation.

#6 Keeping it relatable.

To foster connection and
curiosity my starter questions
are railings on this Tiptoe bridge
something to hold on to
as you explore the text
with yourself
and discuss with others.

As for the answers
there are no right
or wrong answers.

There are only answers
that are honest for you.

Remember
this is not a word for word translation
nor the complete original Torah text.

This is my adaptation lovingly built for
crossing over the fence of Torah

a bridge

high enough
to look over
and close enough
to look within.

May
Tiptoe Through Genesis

be a source
of light and blessing
in your life.

Nancy

In the beginning of
God's creating
the heavens and the earth

when
the earth
was astonishingly
empty

and

darkness
was upon the surface
of the deep

Divine Presence
hovered
over the surface
of the waters.

Genesis 1:1-2

Q. Does God still create? Over "what" or "whom" do you hover?

{From the beginning did God create
the heaven and the earth. And this earth was once confused
and tangled, and darkness was over the turmoil
and a breath of God
hovered over the waters.}
And God said
Let there be light.
And then there was light.

God saw that the light was good
and separated light from darkness
calling to
the light *Day*
and
to the darkness *Night.*

It was evening and it was morning
one day.

Genesis 1:3-5

Q. How can God's Words create light? How do you understand "good"?

God said *Let there be an expanse*
to separate
the waters
from the waters.
And it was so.

God called to the firmament
Heaven.

It was evening and it was morning
a second day.

Genesis 1:6-8

Q. How do you understand heaven? When have you felt the need to separate from some thing, some place or some one?

God said
Let the waters under the heaven
be gathered into one area and let dry land
appear.
And it was so.

God called to the dry land *Earth*
and to the waters *Seas.*

God saw that it was good.

God said *Let the earth sprout vegetation.*
Herbage yielding seed, fruit trees yielding fruit
Each after its kind, each containing its own
seed on the earth.

And it was so.
The earth brought forth
vegetation and herbage yielding seeds
and trees bearing fruit with seeds.

And God saw that it was good.

It was evening and it was morning
a third day.

Genesis 1:9-13

Q. How does Nature reveal the Divine? What do you see when you look
for "good" in your day?

Tiptoe Through Genesis

God said *Let there be two luminaries*
in the expanse of the heaven
to shine upon the earth
and serve as signs for festivals, days and years.
And God made
the greater luminary to dominate the day
the lesser, the night.

And the stars.

And God saw that it was good.

It was evening and it was morning
a fourth day.

Genesis 1:14-19

Q. How do you feel when you look at the sun, moon and stars?
What provides rhythm for your life?

God said *Let the waters*
teem
with living beings which move and let
fowl fly over the earth across
the expanse of the heavens. And God
created sea creatures and creepers
and winged fowl of every kind.

And God saw that it was good.
God blessed them
Be fruitful and multiply.

It was evening and it was morning
a fifth day.

Genesis 1:20-23

Q. How do you understand blessings? How do you measure your daily successes?

Tiptoe Through Genesis

God said *Let the earth bring forth living creatures, each according to its kind; animals, creeping things and land beasts.* And God created them and saw they were good.

God said *Let us make man
with our image and likeness.
They shall rule
over the living creatures and the whole earth.*
And God created man in God's image.
In the image of God
male and female
God created them.

God blessed them *Be fertile and multiply.
Fill the earth and subdue it and rule over all
the living in the waters, the skies and the land.*

God said *Behold I have given you
seeds for all vegetation and trees.
These are foods for you and the
animals and birds.
These are foods for every living soul.*
And it was so.
Indeed, God saw all that God had made
and it was very good.

And it was evening and it was morning
the sixth day.

Genesis 1:24-31

Q. How is creating humans an act of Divine love? In what ways are all humans created equal?

Thus the heaven
and the earth
and all their hosts
were finished in six days.

By the seventh day
God completed the work God had begun.

God ceased
from the creating work
on the seventh day.

God blessed
the seventh day
and
declared it holy
by ceasing the work
God had done before.

Genesis 2:1-3

Q. Why is the Sabbath a blessing? What, for you, makes time holy?

These are the developments of the
heaven and the earth when they were
created on the day of the making {by}
the Lord, God the earth and the heaven.

When God made the heaven and the
earth there were no trees or herbs for
there

had yet to be rain from God
or man to work the ground.

A mist
rose up from the earth and watered
the ground.

And God formed man
from the dust of the ground
and blew into his nostrils
the soul of life

and man
became
a living being.

Genesis 2:4-7

Q. Are you a "body with a soul" or a "soul with a body"?
How do you feel when you consciously breathe deeply?

God planted a garden in Eden
and placed there the man
God had formed.
And God caused every tree
to sprout from the ground.
Each pleasant to look at and good to eat
including the Tree of Life
in the middle of the garden
and
the Tree of Knowledge of Good and Bad.

A river flowed out of Eden
to water the garden
then it divided and was the head of four rivers.

God
placed the man
in the garden in Eden
to work it
and guard it.

Genesis 2:8-15

Q. Compare "Good and Bad" to "Good and Evil". What do you guard?

Tiptoe Through Genesis

{God placed the man God had formed
in the garden in Eden to work it and guard it.}

God commanded the man saying
You may freely eat
of all the trees in the garden
but
from the Tree of Knowledge of Good and Bad
do not eat
for on the day you eat of it
you shall definitely die.

Genesis 2:16-17

**Q. How do you understand the "Tree of Knowledge of Good and Bad?"
How do you like free choice?**

{God placed man in the garden in Eden.}

God said
*It is not good for man to be alone.
I will make him
a helper corresponding to him.*

And God brought
every one of God's creatures
to the man
to name them.
And the man
named them all
but he did not find
a helper corresponding to him.

Genesis 2:18-20

Q. What is the difference between being alone and lonely? How are relationships based on helping?

{In God's garden the man named all the animals but he did not find a helper corresponding to him.} Then God cast a deep sleep upon the man and took from one of his sides then closed the flesh in its place.

God built up that side of man into a woman and God brought her to the man.

And the man said, "This one
at last
bone of my bone, flesh of my flesh. This one shall be named Woman for she was taken from man."

Therefore a man leaves his father and his mother and clings to his wife and they become one flesh. And the two of them were naked and not ashamed.

Genesis 2:21-25

Q. How do men and women complement each other? What does it mean to be "not ashamed"?

Now the serpent
was the most cunning
of all the wild beasts that God had made.
He said to the woman
"Did God really say
you are not to eat from any tree of the garden?"

She said
"God said {that} we can eat the fruit
from all the trees except
the tree in the middle of the garden. God said *You shall not
eat it nor even touch it
lest you die.*"

The serpent said, "Surely you will not die
for God knows that on the day you eat from it
your eyes will be opened
and you will be like God
knowing Good and Bad."

Genesis 3:1-5

Q. How do you understand "the serpent"? By what criteria do you
evaluate a tempting offer?

{The serpent said to the woman "You will not die when you eat of the tree. Your eyes will be like God, knowing Good and Bad."}

And the woman perceived
that
the tree was good for eating
a delight to the eyes
and a means to wisdom.

She took its fruit and ate then gave
some to her husband and he ate
and

opened

were both of their eyes
and they realized
they were naked.

They sewed together fig leaves
to cover themselves.

Genesis 3:6-7

Q. Describe your feelings about your body. How do perceptions impact your decisions?

{The man and woman} heard the sound of God
in the garden and hid.
God called to man *Where are you?*

The man said, "I hid in fear because I am naked."

God said
Who told you that you are naked?
Did you eat from the tree
you were commanded not to eat?

The man said, "The woman you gave me gave me the fruit of
the tree and I ate it." God said to the woman *What have you*
done?

The woman said, "The serpent seduced me
and I ate it."

Genesis 3:8-13

Q. What is the effect of humans realizing their nakedness? Do you hold
yourself accountable for your actions or do you blame others?

Tiptoe Through Genesis

God said to the {seducing} serpent
Because you did this
cursed are you
more than
all the animals and wild beasts.
On your belly
you shall crawl
and dust
you shall eat
all the days of your life.

Hatred I will place
between you and the woman
and between your offspring and her offspring.
Man will strike on your head
and you will strike his heels.

Genesis 3:14-15

Q. How do you understand consequences and God? When have you felt hatred placed upon you?

God said to the woman
{who ate from God's forbidden tree}

*I will greatly increase
your suffering*

and

*childbirth
will be painful.*

*Yet
you will crave your husband
and he will rule over you.*

Genesis 3:16

**Q. How unique is human suffering? How can cravings allow someone to
rule over you?**

Tiptoe Through Genesis

{After God cursed the serpent and woman}
God said to the man
Because you listened to the voice of your wife
and ate from the tree
I specifically told you
was forbidden

the ground beneath you will be cursed
and you will suffer
by the sweat of your brow
to eat its bread
until the day
you return to the ground.

You are dust
and to dust
you shall return.

The man named his woman
Eve
mother of the living.

And God made them clothing.

Genesis 3:17-21

Q. What about work makes you suffer? What importance do you attach to clothes?

God said
Now that man has become like one of us
knowing good and bad
he might reach out
and take also from the Tree of Life
and live forever!

So God expelled man from the garden in Eden
to work the ground from which he came.

God banished away the man and
God stationed the Cherubim {angels} east of Eden along with
the flame of the ever-turning sword to guard the way to the
Tree of Life.

Genesis 3:22-24

Q. What is the problem with humans knowing "good and bad"? How is
each day a present?

{God banished the man and woman}
from the garden in Eden.}

Now the man had known his wife Eve
and she conceived
and gave birth to Cain saying
"I have acquired a man with God."
Then
again
she gave birth
to his brother Abel.

Abel
became a shepherd.

Cain
was a worker of the soil.

Genesis 4:1-2

Q. How do you understand birth and God? How do you feel about what
you "do" with your days?

In the course of time
Cain brought
from the fruit of the ground
an offering to God.
His brother Abel
also brought
from the firstlings of his flock
the choicest
among them.

God
turned to Abel
and his offering
but to Cain and his offering
God did not turn.

Genesis 4:3-5

Q. What makes an offering pleasing to God? How do you handle
rejection?

{After the brothers' offerings
God turned to Abel and not Cain.}
This distressed Cain greatly
and his countenance fell.

God said to Cain
Why are you so angry and depressed?
Surely if you improve yourself
you will be forgiven.

But
if you do not improve yourself
sin crouches at your door
seducing
your desires
still
you can conquer it.

Genesis 4:5-7

Q. In what ways does sin crouch at your door? How does improving oneself bring forgiveness?

{After the brothers' offerings God turned to Abel
not Cain. God said to him *Improve yourself to be forgiven.*
If not, sin crouches towards you.
Still you can conquer it.}

Later
Cain said something
to his brother Abel.

Then
when they happened
to be in the field
Cain rose up against his brother Abel
and killed him.

God asked Cain
Where is your brother Abel?

Cain said
"I do not know.
Am I my brother's keeper?"

Genesis 4:8-9

Q. Why does Cain kill Abel? Are you your brother's keeper?

God said to Cain
What have you done?
The voice
of your brother's blood screams out
to Me from the ground.
Now you are cursed
from the ground.

When you work
the ground
it will no longer
give you its strength.

You will be a restless wanderer.

Genesis 4:10-12

Q. Do the voices of victims still scream out to God? What does it mean to be a restless wanderer?

{After Cain killed Abel, God cursed the ground
to withhold from him
its strength.
God said *You will be a restless wanderer.*}
And Cain said
"My sin is too great to bear.
You have banished me.
I am to be hidden from your Presence.
And whoever finds me
will kill me."

God said
*Whoever kills you will be punished
seven times more.*
Then God put a mark on Cain so no-one
would kill him
and Cain left God's Presence
and settled east of Eden.

Cain knew his wife and they had a son Enoch.
Cain named the city he built, Enoch, after his son.
And Cain had many descendants.

Genesis 4:13-24

Q. How can you be "hidden from God's Presence"? How do you bear
your sins?

Adam knew his wife Eve again and they had a son they
named Seth saying, "God granted me a son in place of Abel
whom Cain had killed."

Adam lived 800 years after Seth was born.
He had sons and daughters.

A son was born to Seth
and he was named Enosh.
It was then
that man began to
to proclaim in the Name of God.

Genesis 4:25-26

Q. How do you express gratitude? How do you move on after loss?

This is the book of the chronicles of man.
On the day that God created man
God made him in the likeness of God.
God created them male and female.
God blessed them and named them Man
on the day that they were created.

Genesis 5:1-2

Q. In what ways are humans made in the likeness of God? Can a person "re-create" him or herself?

Tiptoe Through Genesis

When Adam had lived 130 years
he begot in his image and likeness Seth.
Adam lived 912 years.

{Ten generations from Adam}
Lemekh had a son.
He named him Noah saying
"This one will bring us relief from our work
and the anguish of our hands from the
ground that God has cursed."

Lemekh lived 777 years.
{During that time} man began to increase on the face of the
earth and daughters were born to them.

When the sons of God
took from the daughters of man whomever they chose God
said *My Spirit will not contend evermore concerning Man
since he is but flesh.
His days of life shall be {shortened to} 120 years.*

The sons of God and the daughters of man
fathered the titans
who were on the earth in those days and later.
They were the mightiest
men who ever existed.

Genesis 5:3-6:4

Q. How do you interpret "mightiest men"? How do you feel about your name?

{Many generations after
Adam and Eve}
God saw
man's wickedness
was increasing on earth.

Every
impulse
of man's innermost heart
was
for evil
all
day
long.

Genesis 6:5

Q. What does God see on earth today? What is evil to you?

{God saw human wickedness increasing
and man's innermost thoughts pursuing evil all day long.}
And God
reconsidered
having made Man on earth
with a sad
aching heart.

God said *I will wipe out the Man*
whom I created
from the face of the earth
from man
to cattle
to creeping things
and birds of the sky
for I regret that I have made them.

But Noah
found favor in the eyes of God.

Genesis 6:6-8

Q. How does a human find favor in the eyes of God? What do you regret?

These are the chronicles of Noah.

Noah
was a righteous man
pious
in his generation.
With God
did Noah
walk.

Noah 6:9

Q. What does it mean to be a righteous person? How does "your generation" influence you?

{Righteous man} Noah fathered three sons,
Shem, Ham and Japeth.
Now
the earth had become corrupt before God
and filled with crime.
It was corrupted
for all flesh had perverted its ways.

And God said to Noah
The earth is filled with their crime.
I will thus destroy them with the earth.
Make for yourself an ark out of gopher wood
with compartments.
Construct the ark in cubits 300 (L) x 50 (W) x 30 (H).
A window you will make for the ark.
And to a cubit finish it above.
Put the entrance of the ark on its side,
make it with a bottom, second and third floor.

Behold!
I am about to bring the Floodwaters
to destroy everything with the breath of
life But I will establish with you My
Covenant that you will come into the ark
along with your three sons, wife and the wives of your sons.

Noah 6:10-18

Q. Can all righteous people hear God? How does corruption affect you?

{God told righteous man Noah to build an ark to survive the coming Floodwaters.}

God said *From all life*
take of all flesh
two of each
according to its kind
and bring them to the ark to keep alive with you.
They shall be male and female.

From every species
from every bird, every animal
every creeping creature
two
shall come to you
to keep alive with you
so gather in food
for you and for them.

Noah did everything
exactly
as God
commanded him.

Noah 6:19-22

Q. Are you available for whatever God might ask of you? When are you motivated to "be exact"?

{Noah did everything exactly as God commanded.} God said
to Noah

Come to the Ark, you and all your household
for it is you
that I have seen
be righteous before Me
in this corrupt generation.

Take seven pairs of every clean animal
and two pairs of unclean animals
and seven pair of birds.
For each, take every male and its mate.

For in another seven days it will rain
for forty days and forty nights and I
will obliterate every living thing.

And Noah did all that God commanded.

Noah was 600-years-old when
the Floodwaters came upon the earth.
Noah and his family entered the ark
then the clean and not clean land animals and birds.
All that walked the earth
came two by two to Noah, to the ark.
They were male and female
just as God commanded Noah.

Noah 7:1-9

Q. If there is an ark available for the righteous, what kind would it be?
How do you prepare for endings?

{Noah and all the living left on earth are inside
the ark God told Noah to build.}
Seven days passed
and all the wellsprings of the great deep
burst forth
and the Floodgates
of heaven opened.

And it would continue to rain
upon the earth for forty days and forty nights.

In broad daylight, Noah came with his three sons and their
wives into the ark. They and every land beast of every kind,
every animal, every creeping thing and every bird after its
kind
came to Noah into the ark. They came two
by two all flesh in which there was a breath
of life. Thus they came
male and female
just as God commanded Noah.

And God shut the door on his behalf.

Noah 7:10-16

Q. Has God ever "shut a door" on your behalf? Where do you take
refuge?

Tiptoe Through Genesis

{God sealed righteous Noah and all the living inside the ark.}

When the Floodwaters were
on the earth forty days
the waters strengthened
lifting the ark
and setting it adrift
upon the surface of the waters.
Waters
surging so high
even the highest mountains
were covered by water.
And
all flesh
breathing the spirit of life
everything on dry land
from creeping thing to the birds of the heavens
all
were blotted
out of existence.
Only Noah survived
and those with him in the ark.

Noah 7:17-23

Q. How do you understand natural disasters? When have you felt "adrift"?

{Only righteous Noah
and those with him in the ark survived God's Floodwaters.}

The waters surged on earth for 150 days.

Then
God remembered Noah
and all the animals with him in the ark.

{And} God caused
a wind to blow over the earth
and
the waters
began to subside.

Noah 7:24-8:2

Q. Is there a relationship between God and weather? When have you felt remembered?

{God's Floodwaters of heaven opened
to destroy all the living.
Later God remembered Noah and
the Floodwaters began to subside}.

And after ten months
the mountains became visible.

After forty {more} days
Noah opened the window
and sent out a raven
to see if the land was dry
then later
a dove.
But there was no place to rest their feet
and they returned to the ark.

After seven more days
Noah sent the dove out again
and in the evening
the dove returned to him
with a freshly plucked olive leaf in its beak.

After seven more days
Noah sent the dove out again and this time
the dove did not return.
In time
the land was completely dry.

Noah 8:3-14

Q. How do you understand "time"? Describe yourself when you are
waiting.

{And God's Floodwaters so subsided
that the time came}
when Noah removed the ark cover and he saw the land
was completely dry.

God spoke to Noah
*Go forth from the ark
you and your wife, your sons and your son's wives.
Take with you
every living creature of flesh
all the birds and all the land animals
that walk the earth.
Go out upon the earth
and be fruitful and multiply.*

*Noah left the ark with his family.
Every beast, every animal and every bird
all that walked the land
left the ark
by their families.*

Noah 8:15-19

Q. How can God help you with "a fresh start"? Who gives you the most "second chances"?

Tiptoe Through Genesis

{After leaving the ark}
Noah built an altar to God
and made offerings of clean livestock and birds.

God smelled the pleasing aroma and
God said in God's Heart
Never again
will I curse the ground because of man
for
the inclination of man's heart
is bad from his youth.

Never again
will I destroy
as I just did
all life at once.
Continuous shall be the seasons
the days and nights shall not cease.

Noah 8:20-22

Q. How do you understand "the inclination of man's heart being bad from his youth"? What "continuity" brings you comfort?

{On dry land and out of the ark
Noah made offerings to God and God was pleased.}

God blessed Noah and his children and said
Be fruitful and multiply and fill the earth.
All living things shall fear you
but in your hands
in your care
are they given.

Every living thing that moves
shall be food for you. Like plant vegetation
I have given you everything.
But flesh {of a living creature}
with blood still in its soul
you shall not eat.

Noah 9:1-4

Q. How has God given humans everything we need? How do you
approach food and eating?

{On dry land God continued
saying to Noah and his children}

Of your blood
which belongs to your soul
I will demand an account.

Of every beast
I will demand it
but
man
every man
must account for his brother
for I will demand
the soul of man.

Noah 9:5-6

**Q. How does God demand the soul of humans? How do you "account"
for others?**

{God said to Noah and his children *Every man must account*
for his brother as I will demand the soul of man} *for it is*
in the image of God
God made man.
Whoever sheds the blood of man
by man
shall his blood be shed
for in God's image
God made man.

Now go be fruitful and multiply.
Spread through the earth and hold sway over it.

Noah 9:6-7

Q. Why does God care about the shedding of human blood?
Do you treat others as is if they were also made in the image of God?

Tiptoe Through Genesis

{On dry land God blesses Noah and his children and
demands accountability from all
creatures.} God said to Noah and his
sons with him *As for Me*
I am establishing My Covenant with you and your offspring
after you and with all the living creatures who left the ark.

I will remember My Covenant with you.

Never again
will Floodwaters destroy all the earth.
As a sign
of My eternal Covenant with you
I have placed My rainbow in the clouds.

When I see My rainbow
I will recall the Covenant that exists
between Me, you and every living soul on earth.

Noah 9:8-17

**Q. How do you understand 'all living souls' sharing God's Covenant?
How do you feel about rainbows?**

{After the Flood
the sons of Noah who came out of the ark
were Shem, Ham and Japeth.
From all of them came the earth's populations.

Noah began to be a man of the soil and planted
a.vineyard. Noah
debased himself.
He drank enough wine to make himself drunk
and uncovered himself in the tent.

Ham, the father of Canaan, saw
his father naked
and went outside and told his brothers.
Shem and Japeth then took a cloak
and walking backwards
they covered their father's nakedness.
They faced away and did not see their father naked.

When Noah awoke and found out what his
youngest son had done, he said, "Cursed is
Canaan to be a slave of slaves to his
brothers. Blessed is God, the God of Shem."

Noah 9:18-25

Q. How considerate are you when disclosing information about others?
What does it mean to debase yourself?

{On dry land} the families of Noah's sons are chronicled.
For it was from them
that the nations spread over the earth.

The entire earth
was only of one language
and common purpose.

One human said to another "Let us build us a city and a tower
with its top in the heavens. Let us make a name for ourselves
lest we be scattered across the whole earth."

When God saw
what people with one language built
God confused their language
so they would no longer understand each other.

God named the city Babel
and God scattered humans
across the face of the earth.

Noah 10:1-11:9

Q. What makes these human goals unappealing to God? With whom do you have the most misunderstandings?

{Eighteen generations after the tower in Babel
from the line of Noah's son Shem}
came Nachor whose son
Terach was 70 years old when he fathered
Abram, Nachor and Haran.
Haran had a son Lot. Later, Haran died.

Abram got married as did Nachor.
Abram's wife was Sarai. And Sarai was barren.
She had no child.

Terach took his son Abram,
his grandson Lot and his daughter in law Sarai
and left Ur Casdim heading toward
the land of Canaan.
They came as far as
Charan and settled there.
Terach died in Charan.

Noah 11:10–11:32

Q. How do you describe the people in your family? When have you only
been able to go 'so far'?

Tiptoe Through Genesis

God said to Abram
Go forth from your land, from your birthplace
and from your father's house to a land that I will show you.

I will make your name great
and you shall be a blessing.

I will bless all those who bless you
and curse those who curse you.
All the families of the earth
shall be blessed through you.

Abram went forth as God directed him
when he was 75 years old.

Abram took everything he owned
his wife Sarai and their nephew Lot
and went to the land of Canaan
where the Canaanites lived.

God appeared to Abram and said *This is the land I give you*
and your offspring.
And so Abram built an altar there
to God Who appeared to him.

From there he went to the mountains east of BethEl and built
an altar there and proclaimed in God's Name.

Lech Lecha 12:1-9

Q. How many ways of understanding God are there? What motivates you to change?

{After a time} famine came to the land of Canaan
and Abram, his wife Sarai, and their nephew Lot left
for Egypt. Before they were about to enter, Abram said
to Sarai, "Look. You are a beautiful woman. The men here
will kill me to take you for a wife so pretend you are my
sister." And Sarai did. And Sarai was seen as beautiful and
she was praised to Pharaoh and taken to his palace. He
treated {her brother} Abram to many gifts of silver, gold,
livestock and flock.

God struck Pharaoh and his palace with great plagues
because of Sarai. Pharaoh summoned Abram
"How could you do this to me and say she
was your sister? Take your wife and go."
So, sent away was Abram with
his wife and all that he had {brought and been given}.

Abram went home now
very rich with livestock and silver and gold.
He went by way of the altar in BethEl
{the one} he had made before
for God
and proclaimed in God's Name.

Lech Lecha 12:10-13:4

Q. Do you believe God sends personal plagues for specific reasons?
When have you resorted to a lie?

Tiptoe Through Genesis

{Abram was very rich now with livestock, silver and gold. He, along with his wife Sarai, and his nephew Lot, who also had cattle, sheep and tents headed to the Negev.}

Their wealth was so great
the land could not support them all.
Abram said to Lot
"Let's not
have conflict
between me and you
or among our herdsmen.
After all
we are kinsmen.

All the land is before you.
If you go to the left
I will go to the right
and if you go to the right
I will go left."

Lot looked at the entire plains of Jordan
and it was like God's own garden. Lot chose the lush plains of
Jordan and the two separated.

Lech Lecha 13:5-11

Q. How do you choose between a "relationship" and "material" gain?
What are ways to prevent conflict in your life?

Abram lived in Canaan
while {his nephew}
Lot
went to live in Sodom
where people were very wicked
and sinned against God.

After {Lot} left
God said to Abram
Raise your eyes and look to the north
to the south
to the east and the west.
Rise and walk
the length and breadth of the land
for I will give it all to you.

There Abram built an altar to God
and settled in the plains of Mamre in Hebron.

Lech Lecha 13:12-18

Q. What makes this land so valuable? What is the best gift you ever
received?

Tiptoe Through Genesis

During a war of five kings against four kings
in Sodom and Gomorrah the victor seized
Sodom's spoils and captured Abram's nephew
Lot and others.

When Abram heard, he gathered his
fighting men divided them and attacked that
same night! And Lot, the people and all their
goods were rescued.

So the King of Sodom went to welcome Abram
as did Malki Tzedek, King of Salem who brought bread and
wine. He was a priest to God, Most High. He blessed Abram
"As a priest of God
blessed be Abram to God, Maker of heaven
and earth Who has delivered your enemies
into your hands." And Abram gave him one-tenth
of everything.

The King of Sodom said, "Give me the people
and you keep the goods."

And Abram said, "I lift up my hand to God Most High
Maker of heaven and earth.
Not a thread, nor a shoelace will I take from you
so never can you say 'I made Abram rich.'
Only what all the men have eaten and, for the three men
who went with me, let them take their share."

Lech Lecha 14:1-24

Q. How do you understand Abram's responses to the two kings? Have you ever refused an offer of money or valuables?

After these events
God's Words came to Abram in a vision, saying
Fear not Abram
for I am a shield for you.
Your reward is very great.

Abram said, "O Lord God
what can You give me
seeing as I am childless?"
Suddenly
God's Words came to him.
God said
You shall have a son from your own loins.

Then God took Abram outside and said
Look at the sky and see if you can count the stars.
That is how numerous your descendants will be.
And Abram believed in God
and God reckoned it as righteousness.

Lech Lecha 15:1-6

Q. How does belief in God reckon to God as righteousness? What rewards motivate you?

{Abram believed in God's Words of a future son and many descendants.} God said to him *I am God Who brought you out of Ur to give you this land to inherit.*

Abram said, "My God, how shall I know I am to inherit this land?" God told him to set upon an unlit altar halves of prime pieces of meat. Abram did and kept them safe from the birds of prey. As the sun was about to set, a deep sleep fell upon him and behold – a dread! Great darkness! God said to him *Know with certainty that your offspring shall be strangers in a land not their own – and they will serve them and oppress them for 400 years. But I will judge their oppressors and set your nation free and with great wealth. You shall be buried in peace, at a good old age, and your fourth generation will return here.*

Now as it happened the sun set and it was very dark. Behold –a smoky furnace and a fire torch passed between the prime meat pieces upon the altar.

On that day, God made a pact with Abram. God said *To your descendants have I given this land from the Egyptian river to the Euphrates.*

Lech Lecha 15:7-21

Q. Do you seek confirmation from God? What do you know "with certainty"?

{Now} Abram's wife Sarai
had not borne him any children.
And Sarai had an Egyptian maidservant
named Hagar.
Sarai said to Abram
"God restrains me from having children
so try with my maidservant and I will be built up
through her."
Abram heeded Sarai.
And Sarai gave Hagar to her husband
as a {maidservant} wife
and she conceived.

Afterwards
Hagar acted as if Sarai was no longer important
and her self-esteem was lowered.

She went to Abram, "This is all your fault.
I put my maidservant in your
arms and now that she is pregnant
she looks at me with disrespect.
Let God judge
between me and you."

Abram said
"Your servant is in your hands.
Do with her as you see fit."

Sarai dealt harshly with Hagar and Hagar ran away.

Lech Lecha 16:1-6

Q. How do other people impact your feelings about yourself? How do
you make other people feel important or unimportant?

An angel of God found Hagar by a spring of water in the desert and said *From where are you coming and to where are you going?*

She said, "I am running away from my mistress Sarai."

The angel said
Return and submit to Sarai.
I shall make your family so large
you will not be able to count it.

You will conceive and have a son. Name him Ishmael for God has heard your suffering.

Lech Lecha 16:7-11

Q. When have you been "found" by an angel? Do you know "from where you are coming and to where you are going?"

{An angel of God said to Hagar *Name your son Ishmael for God has heard your suffering.*}

Ishmael will be a rebel
and have his hand against every man
and every man's hand against him.
Still
he will dwell in the face of his brothers.

Hagar said, "You are God of Vision" and named the place
"The Well of the Living One Who Appeared To Me"

Hagar bore a son to 86 year-old Abram
who named him Ishmael.

Lech Lecha 16:12-16

Q. What does God of Vision mean to you? How would you describe
your hand "towards" every man?

Abram was 99
when God appeared to him.

God said

I am All-Sufficing.

Walk before Me and
and become
complete.

*I am ready
to make My Covenant with you
and I will increase your numbers greatly.*

And Abram fell upon his face.

Lech Lecha 17:1-3

Q. How is God All-Sufficing? When do you feel complete?

God continued saying to Abram
In My Covenant
your name shall not be Abram
but Abraham
the father of a multitude of nations.
Kings will descend from you.

I will be God Almighty
to you and to your children for all generations
and
you shall have the land of Canaan
as an everlasting possession.

Lech Lecha 17:4-8

Q. Why does God choose Abram? When have you been offered a true change in your life?

Tiptoe Through Genesis

{In God's Covenant
God is Almighty
to Abraham, father of nations and kings
who will inherit the land of Canaan.}

*As a sign of My Covenant
you shall circumcise
the flesh of the foreskin of all males
now and when
a baby boy is eight days old.*

*Circumcision shall be
the seal of the Covenant between Me and you.
Thus My Covenant shall forever be in your flesh.*

*An uncircumcised male invalidates My
Covenant and his soul shall be cut off from
his people.*

Lech Lecha 17:9-14

Q. How do you express your loyalty to God? What is the status of this Covenant today?

{In God's Covenant
God is Almighty
to Abraham, father of nations and kings
who will inherit the land of Canaan.}

God said to Abraham
Tell Sarai her name will now be Sarah.
I will give her a son through you
and bless her
to be the mother of entire nations.
Kings will be her descendants.

Abraham laughed, saying to himself "How can a 100-year-old man and a 90-year-old {barren} woman have a baby?"

Lech Lecha 17:15-17

Q. When do you talk to yourself? What would you do as a father or mother of a nation?

Tiptoe Through Genesis

{After God told Abraham that kings would descend from his barren wife Sarah} he said to God, "May you grant Ishmael {my son with my maidservant wife Hagar} continued life."

God said *Call Sarah's son Isaac. I shall bless him to keep My Covenant with all his children for eternity.*

I heard your plea for Ishmael. I shall bless Ishmael and make him fruitful increasing his numbers greatly.

Ishmael will father twelve princes and I will make him into a great nation. But I will keep My Covenant with Isaac whom Sarah will bear to you this time next year.

Lech Lecha 17:18-21

Q. What makes a nation great? When have you pleaded to God?

When God finished speaking with {Abraham}
God went up and left him.

That very day, in keeping with God's
Covenant 99-year-old Abraham circumcised
himself his 13-year-old son Ishmael and all the
males in his household.

Lech Lecha 17:22-27

Q. Would Abraham seal this Covenant if he had any doubts about God?
Why do you need to "seal" a deal?

God appeared to Abraham in the heat of the day as he sat
outside his tent. He lifted his eyes and lo! Three strangers!

He perceived them
then ran to them and said, "Come, wash
and rest under the tree.
I will bring you bread
and you can refresh your hearts
then journey on."

They agreed
and Abraham and Sarah made a feast.

Vayera 18:1-7

Q. How is a heart refreshed by hospitality? What refreshes you?

{The three strangers agreed to eat with Abraham and a feast was made.} They ate under a tree.

They asked, "Where is your wife Sarah?"

Abraham answered, "In the tent."

One of them said to him, "I will return to you this time next year and Sarah will have a son."

Sarah {whose female cycle was over} heard this and laughed to herself.
"My husband is old. I am worn out. And now my heart's desire is to come true?"

God said *Why did Sarah laugh? Is there anything too wondrous for God? At the designated time I will return and Sarah will have a son.*

Sarah was afraid and denied laughing but Abraham said, "You did laugh".

Vayera 18:8-15

Q. Is there anything too wondrous for God? What is your heart's desire?

Tiptoe Through Genesis

{After eating with Abraham}
the visitors gazed out over Sodom
then
Abraham escorted them out
and on their way.

God thought
Shall I hide from Abraham
what I plan to do to Sodom?
He is about to become a great nation
through which all the nations of the earth
will be blessed.
I know him.
He will teach his children and those that follow
to keep God's Ways
doing charity
and justice.
Then everything
God promised Abraham
can be fulfilled.

Vayera 18:16-19

Q. What teachings do you want to be known for? What does God know you will do?

{Having decided to share the plan with righteous Abraham
God said to him} *The outcry in Sodom is so great and their
sins so grave*
I will descend to see.

Abraham heard and came and stood before God saying
"Will You
God
kill the innocent people
along with the guilty?

I know I am but dust and ash but God what if 50 or 40 or 30
or 20 or 10 righteous people live there?

I dare say too much God
but if you kill the innocent with the guilty
the righteous and wicked will fare alike.

Shall God
the Judge of all the earth
not do justice?"

God said If *I find 10 good people*
I will not destroy Sodom for their sake.

Vayera 18:20-32

Q. Compare the translations: "righteous versus innocent" and "guilty
versus wicked"? Do you speak up on behalf of others who can't speak
for themselves?

Tiptoe Through Genesis

God's angels arrived in Sodom {ready to destroy it if ten
righteous people were not found.} As it happened
Abraham's nephew Lot was at the city gate.
He greeted them and insisted they come to his
home. And they went. He baked them matzah
and they feasted until bedtime. Suddenly a Sodomite mob
converged on Lot's house demanding the visitors. Lot went
out and tried to
appease them
but still they rushed at him until
the angels reached out, pulled Lot inside, then
blinded the mob so they could no longer find
the door. The angels said to Lot, *God sent us
to destroy this place. Go. Gather those you
wish to save.*

Lot convinced his wife and two daughters to leave.
The angels rushed them out. They said
*Flee for your life. Do not look back.
Do not stop or you too will be destroyed!*
And God made sulphur and fire rain down
on Sodom and Gomorrah destroying everything.
And it was when
the sun arose over the earth and Lot arrived in Tzoar
that Lot's wife turned back to look
and she turned
into a pillar of salt.

Vayera 19:1-26

Q. Do God's angels still save and destroy? How can "looking back" be
destructive?

Abraham woke up early in the morning and
hurried back to the place where he had stood
before God and stared at Sodom and Gomorrah.
He saw heavy smoke rising from the earth.
When God destroyed these cities
God had remembered Abraham {for}
God had allowed {his nephew} Lot to escape.

{Now} Lot was afraid to remain in Tzoar and went to
the hills with his two daughters and lived in a cave.
The older girl said to the younger, "Our father is growing old
and there is no other man left in the world {for us}. Come let
us get him drunk and lay with him.
We will then survive through our children."
And they both did.

Lot's eldest daughter had a son she named Moab.
He began the nation of Moab, which exists today.
And his younger daughter had a son she
named Ben-Ami.
He began the nation of Ammon, which exists today.

Vayera 19:27-38

Q. When have you done something in desperation? How does fear
impact your decision-making?

{When Abraham and Sarah went into the land of King
Abimelech, for safety, Abraham had Sarah pretend
she was his sister.}
And the king's officers
took her for the king to wed
but he fell asleep.
And God came to the king in a dream.
You will die because of the woman you took.

But the king had not come near her. He said, "They said she
was his sister. If I did something it was
with an innocent heart and clean hands."

*God said I know the innocence of your heart; therefore I
restrained you from sinning against Me. Return Sarah to
Abraham for he is a prophet. He will pray for your life and
reopen the wombs of your women.*

And the king summoned Abraham to ask why
{he lied}. Abraham said, "I realized the one
thing missing here
is the fear of God and men would kill me to take
my wife. So I told her to be my sister."

And the king gave livestock, servants {and money} to
Abraham, returned Sarah to him and restored Sarah's dignity.
Then Abraham prayed to God and God healed King
Abimelech, his wife and slaves. God unsealed their wombs
so they were able to have children.

Vayera 20:1-18

**Q. How do you understand the power of prayer? Why does God call
Abraham a prophet?**

And God remembered Sarah just as God had promised and Sarah conceived and she gave birth to Abraham's son in his old age!

It happened at the exact time
God had promised him.

Abraham named him Isaac and
circumcised him on the eighth day as
God commanded.

Abraham was 100 years old when Isaac was
born. Sarah said, "God made
laughter for me; whoever hears
will laugh for me. For who
would have even suggested to Abraham
that {his old} Sarah would be nursing!"

Vayera 21:1-7

Q. Does God have a set time for everything? How do you explain medical miracles?

{At the set time
just as God promised Abraham
and his wife Sarah bore Isaac.}

Isaac grew
and on the day he was weaned
Abraham made a great feast.
There
Sarah saw her maidservant Hagar's son
mocking.

Sarah said to {Abraham}
"Drive out
this slave woman with her son
for her son
shall not inherit with my son Isaac."

Vayera 21:8-10

Q. How respectful are you of someone else's joy? How do you mark
meaningful occasions in your life?

{After Sarah's maidservant Hagar's son
mocked her son
she said to Abraham, "Drive out this slave woman with her
son for he shall not inherit with my son Isaac."}

The matter upset Abraham very much but God said
Do not be distressed.
Heed Sarah's voice
for through Isaac
will your seed be acclaimed.
But
the son of the slave woman
I will also make into a nation
for he is your offspring.

{So}
Abraham woke up early and gave {"his maidservant wife"}
Hagar bread and a pouch of water and sent her away with the
boy.

Vayera 21:11-14

Q. How do you prioritize your relationships? Do your priorities affect
your relationships?

{After Abraham sent Hagar away with the boy Ishmael} Hagar
wandered aimlessly in the Beer Sheba desert.
When their water ran out, she put the boy under the bushes
for she did not want to watch him die. And she lifted her voice
and wept loudly.

God heard the boy weeping
and God's angel called to Hagar from heaven
Do not be afraid Hagar.
God hears the boy's cries.
Lift him up and hold him tight
for I will make a great nation of him.

Then God opened her eyes and she saw a
well of water and she filled the pouch and
gave the boy a drink. Thereafter God was
with Ishmael as he grew up in the desert of
Paran
and became an accomplished archer.
His mother arranged an Egyptian wife for him.

Vayera 21:14-21

**Q. When have your "eyes been opened"? What do you do when you feel
helpless?**

{After much dispute}
Abraham settled well-rights in Beer Sheba with seven ewes
as proof he dug the well. And he planted a tamarisk tree there
and proclaimed
the Name of God Eternal
God of all the Universe.

And Abraham sojourned there for many days.

Vayera 21:22-34

Q. Does God being eternal bring you comfort? How do you understand 'God of all the universe'?

Tiptoe Through Genesis

It was after these things
that God tested Abraham.

God said to him *Abraham*.

Abraham said to God, "Here I am."

*God said Take Isaac your son whom you love
and get yourself to the land of Moriah
and offer
him up
on one of the mountains that I will show you.*

Vayera 22:1-2

**Q. How do you know when something is a test from God? What have
you learned from the tests in your life?**

{God tested Abraham. God said *Take Isaac your son whom you love and offer him to Me on the mountain that I will show you.*} Abraham got up early in the morning took wood, servers and Isaac and left for the place where God designated.

After three days Abraham told the servers "Wait here while we go worship."

Abraham gave his son Isaac the wood to hold while he held the slaughtering knife and some fire.

Isaac spoke up, "Father."

Abraham said, "Here I am my son."

Isaac said, "Here is the fire and wood but where is the lamb for the offering?"

Abraham said, "God will provide for God a lamb for the offering."

Vayera 22:3-7

Q. What does faith in God provide? When have you had to trust in God?

{Abraham said to his son Isaac, "God will provide for God a
lamb for the offering."}
And they journeyed to the place
God designated {for Abraham to offer his son}. There
Abraham built the altar, arranged the wood
and bound his son Isaac on top. Abraham stretched forth his
hand and took his knife to slaughter his son
when
an angel of God called from heaven
Abraham! Abraham!

And Abraham said, "Here I am."

God's angel said, *Do not harm him for I
know now that you are a God-fearing man
as you have not withheld from Me your only
son.* And Abraham raised his eyes and saw
– behold!
A ram caught in the branches by its horns.
So Abraham went
and made the offering with the ram instead of his son and
named the site
Hashem Yireh {Jerusalem}
God will see.
Today it is therefore said
"On God's Mountain God will be seen."

Vayera 22:8-14

Q. Are you God-fearing? What does Jerusalem mean to you and to the
world?

Then God's angel called out to Abraham
a second time from heaven saying, *God said*
Abraham
because you did not withhold
your only son from Me
I will bless you and multiply you
so that your offspring
shall be like the stars of the heavens
and sand on the shores of the sea.
Your offspring shall inherit the gate of his enemies.
And all the nations of the earth shall bless
themselves through your descendants
because you
have hearkened to My Voice.

Abraham returned to his servers
and they all went home.

Vayera 22:15-19

Q. What kind of blessings does hearkening to God's Voice bring?
When have you proved your faith?

Tiptoe Through Genesis

Sarah lived until she was 127 years old and died in Hebron.
Abraham eulogized her and withdrew to weep.

Later Abraham rose to buy land for her burial. Ephron, child
of Heth, declined any payment saying, "You are a prince of
God in our midst."

But Abraham insisted on buying it
and paid 400
shekels in front of the city gate
with the locals and all the children of Heth
as eyewitnesses.

Thus, Ephron's field, the cave on it and
every tree within its circumference was
now the uncontested property of Abraham.
He then buried his wife Sarah in the cave
of Machpelah
which adjoins Hebron in the
land of Canaan.

Chaya Sarah 23:1-20

Q. What do you insist upon? How can "free" actually "cost"?

{It was after Sarah's burial}
and Abraham knew
God had blessed him in everything
but he felt old.
He said to his oldest closest servant, "Go find Isaac a wife
and swear by the God of heaven and earth
that you will not take a Canaanite wife.
Go instead to my kinsmen and to my birthplace.
For it is my offspring whom God will give this
land."

The servant said, "And if she does not wish to
follow, will your son go to her?"

Abraham said, "God made an oath
To your offspring
I will give this land.
{So}
God will send you an angel
to help you find a wife for my son.
If she declines, the oath is absolved
for he will not go there."

Thereupon, Abraham's servant took ten camels and many
gifts and journeyed to his master's birthplace in the city of
Nahor.

Chaya Sarah 24:1-10

**Q. Do all oaths involve God? How does the family of your spouse
impact your marriage?**

Tiptoe Through Genesis

{The most trusted servant of Abraham
went to find a wife for Isaac, his master's
son.} When he arrived outside the city
Nahor, he let his ten camels rest on their
knees near the well.
It was evening and around the time women would come to
draw water. He prayed

"God of my master Abraham please grant him a kindness.
Have the girl whom you want to be Isaac's wife give me water
then offer a drink for my camels too."

Chaya Sarah 24:11-14

Q. What qualities do you need from a spouse? What qualities do you
bring to your relationships?

{To find a wife for Isaac
Abraham's servant prayed near the town well for a
maiden to grant him a drink and also offer to water
his camels.} Just then Rebecca appeared.

She was extremely good-looking
and still untouched by any man.
She descended to the well, filled her jug and ascended. The
servant ran towards her asking, "Let me sip, if you please a
little water from your jug?"

She said, "Drink my lord." Then quickly she lowered her jug to
her hand and gave him a drink.

When she finished giving him a drink
she said, "I will draw water
even for your camels and until
all of them have had their fill."

He gazed upon her in wonder as she hurried to pour water in
the troughs then went running back to the well to get water for
his camels.

Chaya Sarah 24:15-21

Q. When given the opportunity, do you initiate a good deed? What is the
value of virginity?

{Abraham's servant was watching
the young maiden who gave him a drink and now watered
his camels with awe.} But he remained silent
waiting to determine for sure whether or not God had
made his journey
{to find the right wife for his master's son}
fully successful.

When the camels finished drinking he
gave her gold jewelry. He said "Whose
daughter are you? Tell me, please is
there a place in your father's home for
us to stay overnight?"

She said, "I am the daughter of Bethuel. We have plenty of
straw and fodder as well as a place for people to spend the
night."

Abraham's servant bowed low before God
"Blessed be God. God of Abraham
Who did not withhold from my master
the loving-kindness
and truth
God has always granted him. Here I
am still on the road and God has led
me to my master's kin."

Chaya Sarah 24:21-27

Q. How would you describe Abraham's God? What does it mean to
practice loving-kindness?

Rebecca went to her mother and shared all that had
happened {at the well} while her brother Laban went to greet
the stranger.

Later her father joined the men for a meal. Abraham's servant
said, "I shall not eat until I have spoken my piece.

God has granted my master {Abraham}
great blessings and prosperity.
He is aging and will {one day}
pass everything to his son. He does not want his son to marry
a Canaanite so he sent me here {to his kinfolk} to find a wife.

They said, "Since this is something from God
so it shall be."

And the servant brought out more gifts of gold and silver
jewelry and clothing
and gave them to Rebecca and also
gave gifts to her brother and mother. And
they feasted.

Chaya Sarah 24:28-54

Q. How do you know when something is "from God"? How do gifts
influence a relationship?

Tiptoe Through Genesis

{It was the morning after the feast when it was agreed
Rebecca would wed Isaac, the son of Abraham.} And
Abraham's servant was now ready to leave with her.
Rebecca's mother and brother wanted her to stay
a little longer but Abraham's servant said "Do not
delay me as God has already shown
my mission to be successful.
Let me leave so I can go to my master."

And so they summoned Rebecca and said
"Do you want to go with this man?"

And she said, "I will go."

The next day Rebecca's family blessed her
"Our sister, may you come
to be thousands of myriads
and your offspring
inherit
the gate of their enemies."
And Rebecca left with her server.

Chaya Sarah 24:54-61

Q. How do you face change? When have you felt successful in a
mission?

{In the Negev area Abraham's son Isaac was on his way home} and towards the evening he went out to meditate in the field.

He raised his eyes and saw camels approaching. When Rebecca looked up and saw him she leaned into her camel and closer to the servant. She said, "Who is this man coming toward us in the field?"

He said, "That is my {master's son}." And Rebecca took her veil and covered herself.

Chaya Sarah 24:62-65

Q. How do you feel about modesty? What is the value of taking time for meditation or prayer?

Upon returning {with Rebecca
Abraham's trusted} servant told
Isaac all that had happened and
Isaac took Rebecca
into his mother's tent.
He married her
and he loved her.
Thus
Isaac was consoled
after the loss of his mother.

Chaya Sarah 24:66-67

Q. How can loving others console you? How unique is every love?

Abraham
took again a wife, Keturah
who bore him children.

Abraham
gave all that he had
to Isaac
{his son with Sarah}.

To his concubines
he gave them gifts
then sent them away from Isaac
while he was still alive.

At 175, Abraham had his last breath
and died satisfied
and was gathered to his people.

Chaya Sarah 25:1-8

Q. Why does Abraham treat his heirs differently? What do you think you
will need to "die satisfied"?

{Abraham died old and satisfied.}

His sons
Isaac and Ishmael
buried him with Sarah {his wife}
in the cave of Machpelah
on the land he had purchased.

After Abraham died
God
blessed
Isaac.

And Isaac
settled near Be'er-lahai-ro'l.

Chaya Sarah 25:9-11

Q. What is Abraham's legacy? Under what conditions do you put family conflicts aside?

These are the chronicles of Ishmael
son of Abraham
whom Hagar the Egyptian, Sarah's maidservant
bore to Abraham.

These are the names of Ishmael sons
in order of their birth:
Nebayoth, Kedar, Adbiel, Mibsam,
Mishma, Duma, Masa, Chadad, Terma, Yetur,
Nafish and Kedman.
There were
twelve princes
for their nations.

Ishmael lived until 137.
He died and was gathered to his people.
His descendants lived in the area from Havilah to Shur
which borders on Egypt
all the way to Assyria, over all his brethren.

Chaya Sarah 25:12-18

Q. What is Ishmael's legacy? How would you describe the chronicles of
your life?

These are the chronicles
of Isaac
son of Abraham {and Sarah}.

At 40 years old
Isaac
married Rebecca
who was unable to conceive.

Isaac pleaded with God for her sake.
And God allowed him to be
convincing.

And
Rebecca conceived.

When Rebecca
felt children clashing inside her
she went to inquire of God.

Toledoth 25:19-22

Q. Where do you go to inquire of God? When has God allowed you to
be convincing?

{When Rebecca felt children clashing inside her
she went to inquire of God.}
God said to her
Two nations are in your womb.

Two kingdoms
will separate
from inside you.

The power
from one kingdom
will pass to the other
and the elder
shall serve the younger.

And behold!
At birth there were twins!
The first one came out red-cheeked and hairy.
They named him Esau.
His brother then emerged smooth-skinned
and his hand was grasping Esau's heel.
They named him Jacob.

Toledoth 25:23-26

Q. How do you feel about power? What have you grasped for?

Tiptoe Through Genesis

{Isaac and Rebecca's twin} boys grew up.
Esau was skilled in hunting
a man of the field.
Jacob was a scholarly man
staying in tents.
Isaac loved Esau
because of the meat he brought from hunting
but Rebecca loved Jacob.

Toledoth 25:27-28

Q. What do you base your love on? How would you describe your
parents and love?

{Isaac and Rebecca's twins
Esau and Jacob grew older.}

Jacob was once simmering a pot of stew
when {his older brother} Esau
came from the fields exhausted.
Esau said to Jacob
"Give me a swallow of that red stuff.
I'm famished."
(Thereafter Esau became known
as Edom {Red}.)

Jacob said, "Sell me today
your birthright blessing."

Esau said, "Indeed I am about to die
so of what use is a birthright to me?"

Jacob said, "Swear an oath to me right now." And Esau
swore to him and sold his birthright to Jacob.

Jacob then gave Esau bread and lentil stew.
Esau ate it, drank, got up and left.
Thus Esau rejected his birthright.

Toledoth 25:29-34

Q. What makes an oath binding? What do you value or reject about your family?

When a famine came to the area God said to Isaac *Stay in
this land of the Philistines and
I will be with you
and bless you
and establish with you
the oath
that I swore to your father Abraham.*

*Your offspring will be
like the stars of the heavens.*

*The nations of the earth
shall bless themselves through you.*

*This is all because
Abraham obeyed My Voice
and kept My Covenant
and Commandments.*

Toledoth 26:1-5

**Q. How are you blessed when others obey God? What motivates you to
obey?**

In the land of the Philistines
Isaac's wealth grew
and the Philistines
became jealous
and plugged his wells dug in the days of Abraham.

The next well brought no quarrels so he
named it Rehoboth, "For now God has
granted us space to be fruitful."

Isaac went up to Beer Sheba where God appeared
to him saying *I am the God of your father Abraham.
Fear not for I am with you. I will bless you and increase your
descendants because of My servant Abraham.*

{There} Isaac built an altar to God and proclaimed God by
Name while his servers dug new wells looking for water.

Later the Philistine king came to Isaac
saying, "We have indeed seen that God is with
you." And there was peace between them and
they feasted. That very day
Isaac's servants found water.
The place is called Beer Sheba to this day.

Toledoth 26:6-33

Q. What is required to achieve peace? How do you handle jealousy?

When Esau was forty
he married two Hittites
who became a source
of spiritual bitterness
to his parents Isaac and Rebecca.

Toledoth 26:34-35

Q. What is spiritual bitterness? What are you "a source of" for your parents?

{Isaac and Rebeca had twins,
Esau and Jacob}
Isaac had grown old
blind and near death.

He summoned his eldest son Esau and said
"My son
I know not the day of my death.
Go hunt and make me the dish I love.
I will eat
and then my soul
will bless you
and you can be granted
your birthright
as my firstborn son."

Listening to Isaac
speak to Esau
was Rebecca.

Toledoth 27:1-27:5

Q. What is your birthright? Do you want to know the day of your death?

{When elder son Esau left to hunt}
Rebecca went to Jacob and said, "My son, listen. I heard your
father speaking to your brother
{about eating his stew, then bestowing the blessing for his
firstborn.} Now fetch two choice goats. I
will make your father Isaac his tasty
dish. Then you will bring it to him so he
shall eat and bless you before death."

Jacob said, "But my brother is hairy and I
am smooth. Suppose father touches me.
He will realize
that I am an imposter
and I will gain a curse
rather than a blessing."

Rebecca said, "Let the curse be on me.
But listen and bring me what I asked."

Toledoth 27:6-13

Q. Can blessings or curses be transferred? When have you made
sacrifices in your life?

{"Let the curse be on me," Rebecca told son Jacob
but go to his father Isaac
disguised as his elder brother Esau to receive his
firstborn blessing.}

So Jacob fetched the goats for the stew and Rebecca made
Esau's stew recipe that her husband Isaac loved. Then she
dressed Jacob
in Esau's best clothing
placed young {hairy} goat skins on his arms and
neck and handed her son the stew.

Toledoth 27:14-16

Q. How willing are you to participate in deception? Have you ever felt
like an imposter?

Tiptoe Through Genesis

{In order to receive Isaac's blessing for the firstborn son Rebecca dressed son Jacob as his elder brother Esau.} Rebecca gave Jacob the stew and the bread she had made. Jacob came to his father and said, "Father."

Isaac said, "Yes. Who are you my son?"

"It is I, Esau, your firstborn," said Jacob. "Eat the stew of my hunt so that your soul may bless me."

Isaac said, "How did your hunt go so quickly my son?"

Jacob said, "Because God, your God, was with me."

"Come closer," said Isaac. "Let me touch you my son. Are you really Esau or not?"

Jacob came closer and Isaac touched him and said, "The voice is Jacob's voice but the hands are the hands of Esau." Isaac did not realize who it was. He said, "Are you really my son Esau?"

And Jacob said, "I am."

Toledoth 27:17-24

Q. Why does Jacob say that God was with him for the hunt? How do you handle doubt?

{Isaac touched his son before him. "Are you really my son
Esau?" And Jacob said to his father, "I am."}

Isaac ate his tasty stew and drank the wine.

Then Isaac asked for Esau to come kiss him and Jacob went.
Isaac smelled his garments then blessed him saying
"The smell of my son
is the smell of the fields that God has blessed.
May God
grant you the dew of the heavens and
the fatness of the earth, abundant with grain and wine.

Nations will serve you and kingdoms will bow to you. You
shall be like a lord to your brothers and to you
your mother's children will bow. Cursed
be they who curse you and blessed be
they who bless you."

Toledoth 27:25-29

Q. How have those who have blessed and cursed Isaac's descendants
fared over time? Describe what is abundant in your life.

Tiptoe Through Genesis

{Disguised as his elder brother Esau Jacob went and received their father's blessings for the firstborn son.}

And
Jacob departed
just as his brother
returned from his hunt.

Esau came to his father with the stew he had prepared. He said, "Let my father get up and eat his son's stew so that your soul may bless me."

Isaac said, "Who are you?"

Esau said, "I am your firstborn son Esau."

Isaac was seized with a violent fit of trembling "Who then brought me the stew I ate? Who did I bless? Indeed he shall remain blessed!"

Esau heard his father's words and he let out a most loud and bitter scream crying out "Bless me too, Father!"

Toledoth 27:30-34

Q. Can blessings or curses be taken back? How final are your decisions?

{Esau let out a loud and bitter scream and pleaded "Bless me too, Father!"}

Isaac said, "Your brother came with deceit
and took your blessing."

Esau said, "Did you name him Jacob meaning the heel so
that he should twice trip me by the heels? He took away my
birthright and see now my blessings!" Esau wept, "Father
have you no blessing for me?"

Isaac said, "Indeed the fatness of the earth shall be your
dwelling and the dew of the heavens above.
By sword you shall live
and your brother, shall you serve. When you are validly
aggrieved you may cast off
his yoke from upon your neck."

Toledoth 27:35-40

Q. When is a grievance valid? How can a "yoke" be cast off?

Tiptoe Through Genesis

Esau seethed hatred at his younger brother Jacob
{for impersonating him
and receiving his father's blessing
due to him as firstborn son.}

He said to himself, "The days of mourning for my
father will be here soon and then I
will be able to kill my brother."

When {their mother} Rebecca found out
she said to Jacob
"Your brother is consoling himself with
plans to kill you. Now flee to my brother
Laban and remain there
until your brother's anger has subsided.
Why should I lose you both on the same day?"

Toledoth 27:41-45

Q. Does revenge truly console? What subsides your anger?

{When Rebecca discovered her son Esau had plans to kill her other son Jacob she told him to flee to her kin.}

Then Rebecca went to her husband Isaac and said, "I am disgusted at life because Esau's wives {are a source of spiritual bitterness}. I will just die if Jacob weds {Canaanite} Hittites like them."

So Isaac summoned Jacob and said

"Do not marry a Canaanite.

Marry a daughter from your Uncle Laban's family. And may God bless you and make you fruitful and numerous and may you be a congregation of peoples.
May God grant the blessing of Abraham
to you and your offspring
so that you may
possess the land
which God gave him."

Esau heard this and understanding that intermarrying with Canaanite girls was displeasing to his father he married the daughter of Abraham's son Ishmael.

Toledoth 27:46-28:9

Q. What is your spiritual heritage? Who do you try to please or displease?

Jacob fled from his brother Esau
to his uncle's home in Charan.
He encountered a place and spent
the night there because the sun had set.
He picked up some stones and placed
them around his head then lay down in
that place. And Jacob dreamt.

Behold! A ladder was set towards earth and its top
reached toward heaven.
And behold! Angels of God
were going up and down on it.

Suddenly God was standing over him saying
I am the God of Abraham and God of Isaac.
I will give to you and your family this land.

Your offspring
like dust of the earth
will grow and spread.
All the families on earth
will be blessed through you and your descendants.

I will protect you wherever you go.
I will return you to this soil.
And I will keep this promise to you.

Jacob awoke, saying, "Indeed
God is present in this place
and I did not know it."

Vayetze – 28:10-16

Q. How do you understand the ladder in Jacob's dream? What does it take to know "God is present"?

{With stones around his head and God
and angels in his dream, Jacob awoke saying, "Indeed God
is present in this place and I did not know it."}
And he became frightened.
Awed
he exclaimed
"This is
the house of God
the gate of heaven."
Then Jacob stacked the stones into a pillar
poured oil on it and named it BethEl (God's Temple) vowing
"If God will be with me and take care of me
and return me to my father's home in peace
God will be a God to me.

And for all God gives me I will give a tenth {a tithe} to God
and God's Temple."

Vayetze – 28:17-22

Q. How equal is the exchange between what you give God versus what
you receive from God? How do you treat those who "take care" of you?

Jacob lifted his feet towards
the home of his {uncle} Laban. When almost there he came
upon a well in Paran shut tight with a rock. Shepherds were
waiting
until everyone arrived to open the well.
Jacob asked if they knew his uncle. "Look!"
they said "There's his daughter Rachel
coming now." So Jacob
uncovered the well for her
and watered his uncle's sheep.

{Afterwards}
Jacob kissed Rachel and wept aloud as he told her he was
Rebecca's son and thus {marriageable} brethren. And so she
ran to tell her father Laban
who welcomed him as family.

Thereafter Jacob helped with his uncle's flocks until Laban
said to him, "Just because you are a close relative does that
mean you should serve me without compensation? Tell me
what shall your wages be?"

Vayetze – 29:1-15

Q. What does it mean to "welcome someone as family"? How do you
approach money matters with your family?

{Laban offered to pay Jacob for his help with the flocks.}

Laban
had two daughters.
The older one's name was Leah and
the younger one's name was Rachel.

Leah had lovely eyes
while Rachel was shapely and beautiful.

Jacob
had fallen in love
with Rachel
so he said to Laban
"I will work for you
for seven years
for your younger daughter Rachel."

And Laban agreed.

So Jacob worked for seven years for Rachel
though they seemed to him only a few days
because of his love for her.

Vayetze 29:16-20

Q. How do you "fall in love"? When or with whom does "time fly"?

{Jacob worked for Laban for seven years to wed
his youngest daughter Rachel.}
Jacob spoke up, "The time is up. Give me my bride for my
working days have been
completed."

{Agreeing} Laban invited all the local people
and made a wedding feast.
That night
he brought his daughter Leah to Jacob
and the marriage was consummated.
Jacob woke up the morning after the wedding.
Behold!
It was Leah by his side.

Jacob said to Laban
"Why have you deceived me?"

Laban said, "It is our custom that younger
daughters never marry before the elder.
Finish the week with Leah then for Rachel
you shall work another seven years."

Jacob complied
and completed the week with Leah
before Rachel became his wife.

Vayetze 29:21-29

Q. When have you felt the most deceived? What will you do for love?

{Jacob worked his years to marry Rachel
but his father-in-law deceived him into marrying Leah first.}

Jacob
loved Rachel
more than her older sister Leah.

God saw
Leah was unloved
so he opened her womb.

She birthed a son she named Reuben
saying, "God has seen my trouble
and now my husband will love me."

Then she birthed a son she named Simeon
saying, "God has heard I was unloved."

Her third son, she named Levi for "Now
my husband will become attached
saying, I have given him three sons."

Her fourth son she named Judah saying,
"This time let me praise God."

Then she stopped having children.

Vayetze 29:30-35

Q. How do you seek love? Can you control love?

{Jacob is married to sisters Rachel and Leah.}

Rachel saw
that she had not borne children to Jacob
and she became envious
of her sister
{who had given him four sons already}.

Rachel said to her husband Jacob
"Give me children otherwise I'll die."

Jacob was furious
"Is it I
instead of God
who is holding back
the fruit of your womb?"

Vayetze 30:1-2

Q. Who do you blame for what you can't control? How do you handle envy?

{Jacob's anger flared at Rachel,"Is it I, instead of
God Who has withheld from your womb?"}
Rachel said to him
"Take my maidservant Bilbah.
Let her give birth on my lap
so through her
I shall have a son."

Jacob did and Bilbah
bore a son Dan
saying, "God has judged me and heard my prayer"
followed by a son Naphtali
saying, "Through all of God's roundabout ways
I have finally won."

Then Leah gave Jacob her maidservant
Zilpah and she bore a son, Gad saying,
"Good luck has come!" Then a second son,
Asher
saying, "In my happiness
women see me as fortunate."

Vayetze 30:3 -13

Q. When have you experienced God's roundabout ways? How do you
understand "luck"?

{Rachel was barren while her sister Leah
and both of their maidservants had sons by Jacob.}

One day Leah's son Reuben found {fertility} mandrakes.
Rachel said to Leah
"Please, give me some of your son's mandrakes."

Leah said, "Isn't it enough you have taken away my
husband - now you want my son's mandrakes too?"

Rachel said to Leah, "All right. Jacob will sleep with you
tonight in exchange for your mandrakes."

Leah agreed and she was with Jacob.

And God heard Leah's prayers.
She birthed Issachar
saying, "God has given me my reward"
and Zebulun
saying, "God has given me a wonderful gift"
and a girl, Dinah.

Vayetze 30:14-21

Q. Do you feel God "rewards you"? What is best gift you have ever
given?

{Rachel had been barren with her husband Jacob while her
sister and both of their handmaids had all borne him sons.}

Then God remembered Rachel
and hearkened to her prayers.

God opened Rachel's womb
with Jacob
and she gave birth to a son.
Rachel said, "God has gathered away my humiliation."

She named him Joseph
saying, "May God grant another son to me."

Vayetze 30:22-24

Q. Does prayer help God remember? When have you felt your
humiliation be gathered away?

After Rachel gave birth to {Jacob's son} Joseph Jacob went
to his father-in-law. He said, "It is time
for me go to my homeland with my children and my wives for
whom you remember I worked and served."

Laban said, "God blessed me because of you.
Just name your price and I will give it."

Jacob chose the speckled and spotted flock
and after separating them from Laban's flock, he encouraged
mating. Jacob became very wealthy and suddenly
Laban's sons started saying
that Jacob stole from their father.

And when Jacob met with Laban face to face
the tone had changed
and it was not as it was before.

Vayetze 30:25-31:2

Q. How do you feel when other people are successful? How do you
handle a "change of tone" in a relationship?

{The tone had changed with Laban and his sons because of Jacob's success.} God said to Jacob *Go back to your birthplace in the land of your fathers and I will be with you.* {So} Jacob summoned his wives Rachel and Leah to see his flock.

He said, "I served your father well but he has changed my pay at least ten times. If not for God, I would have nothing. Now for my wages, I chose the speckled and spotted flock. Afterwards I had a vision of inspiring mating and tried it. {Then} an angel called to me in God's Name.

I said, 'Here I am.'
{Then} the angel said *I see what Laban is doing to you. I am God of BethEl where you anointed an altar and made an oath to Me. Now set out and leave this land. Return to the land where you were born.*

Rachel and Leah said to him {about leaving their father} "Do we even have a portion in our father's estate? Why, he treats us like strangers! He sold us and spent the money. This belongs to us and our children. Whatever God says to do, do it."

Vayetze 31:3-16

Q. What makes you feel like a stranger? Have you or do you take advantage of family?

Tiptoe Through Genesis

{When the tone changed
between Jacob and his father-in-law Laban
God told Jacob to leave and return home.}

Jacob began the journey by
placing his children and wives {Rachel and Leah}
on the camels. Then he led his livestock and took all the
goods he purchased and headed
to see his father Isaac in the land of Canaan.

{Meanwhile}
when Laban was away sheering sheep.
Rachel stole her father's teraphim idols.

And
Jacob
went around Laban's back
and did not tell him
that he was leaving.
Thus
he fled with all he owned.

Vayetze 31:17-21

Q. With whom do you feel you must protect yourself? Have you ever
gone around someone's back?

It took ten days for Laban to find his daughters
and son-in-law Jacob.
And God came to him in a dream that night
Say nothing good or bad to Jacob.

The next day Laban confronted Jacob "Why did you kidnap
my daughters, deny me my goodbyes and steal my teraphim
idols? Why, we would have sent you off
with celebration and song! But you
didn't even let me kiss my grandchildren goodbye.
I could do you harm
but your God warned me in a dream last night
Say nothing good or bad to Jacob.
{Now} I realize you left because you missed
your parent's home but why did you steal my idols?"

Jacob said, "I was afraid
you would take your daughters from me with force
but whoever took your idols will not live."

Jacob did not know
Rachel had stolen them.

Vayetze 31:22-32

Q. Have you ever felt warned by God? How does refraining from
speaking help relationships?

Laban searched for his {stolen} teraphim
idols in the tents of Jacob {his son-in-law}
then those of his servants
then his daughter Leah's tent then his daughter Rachel's tent.
But, he found nothing for Rachel
had put them in her camel's saddlebag and sat on them.
She said to her father, "Do not be angry for I am in
a womanly way and cannot get up for you."

Afterwards
Laban made a treaty with Jacob
{sealed by} building a mound and monument
and eating together.

Laban said, "With God as witness, do not ever
degrade my daughters or marry others."

Jacob agreed and they feasted.

The next day
Laban kissed his daughters and grandchildren
goodbye. He blessed them and returned home.

Vayetze 31:33-32:1

Q. What do you need from "a goodbye"? How can you degrade someone?

Jacob journeyed towards
the land of Canaan
{where he had long ago
deceived his father Isaac and brother Esau.}

Angels of God encountered him and
when he saw them, Jacob said "This is
a camp of God!"

{Then} Jacob sent messengers
ahead to tell Esau
"Your humble servant Jacob
says
'I have been staying with Laban
and now I am wealthy with livestock, flocks and servers.
I am sending word to gain favor in your eyes.'"

But his messengers returned
and said
"Esau is coming
and with him are 400 men."

Vayetze 32:2-7

Q. In relationships, what helps gain favor in your eyes?
What has humbled you?

{Jacob sent word with his messengers to his brother Esau to
gain favor in his eyes. But Esau was still approaching with
400 men.} Frightened and distressed Jacob divided his
families and livestock into two camps
so if one was struck
he would still have the other.
Jacob prayed
"O God of my father Abraham
God of my father Isaac.
You told me to return home and all would be well.

I am unworthy of all your kindness.
When I left home
I had only my walking staff.
Now I have enough for two camps.

Rescue me, I pray
from the hand of my brother Esau
whom I fear will strike down
me, mothers and children
for You once said
*I will make things go well with you
and your descendants will be
like the sand grains of the sea
too numerous to count.*"

VaYishlach 32:8-13

Q. How worthy are you of God's kindness? When have you needed to
be rescued?

{After praying alone to God for rescue from his approaching brother Esau and his 400 men} Jacob selected generously from a variety of his livestock to give as tributes to his brother.

Then Jacob sent his messengers separately and throughout the night with these gifts to Esau. Jacob told his messengers "When he asks, 'From who?' say 'Your servant Jacob. It is a tribute sent to my lord, to Esau from {Jacob} who is himself right behind us'."

Jacob said to himself "I will send gifts and then I will face him. Hopefully he will forgive me."

And so the tributes continued throughout that night that Jacob spent at the camp.

Vayishlach 32:14-24

Q. How do you understand the process of forgiveness? What does it take to "face" those whom you have hurt?"

{Separated from his family, Jacob sent messengers throughout the night with gifts to his brother Esau who was approaching with 400 men.} Left
alone
was Jacob.
And a man wrestled with him until break of dawn. When he perceived that he could not overcome he struck the socket of Jacob's hip and dislocated it. He wrestled with him and said "Let me go for dawn has broken."

And Jacob said, "I will not let you go unless you bless me."

He said, "No longer is your name Jacob.
Your name shall be Israel
for you have striven with the Divine
and with man
and have overcome."

Jacob named the place Peniel for "I have
seen the Divine face to face yet my life
was spared." And Jacob limped away.
To this day, the Children of Israel are not to eat
from an animal's hip socket area.

Vayishlach 32:25-33

Q. What does it mean to strive with the Divine and man? When has your life been spared?

When Jacob could see Esau and his 400 men approaching
he put behind him the handmaids and their children then
Leah and her children and then Rachel and Joseph in back.

{Then} Jacob went forward
bowing seven times until he drew near his brother.
Esau ran to embrace him and they wept.
He said, "Who are all these people?"

Jacob said, "These are the children
God favored upon your servant."
And all the women and children bowed.

Esau said, "But why all these gifts?"

Jacob said, "To find favor in your eyes."

Esau said, "I have much my brother, keep what is yours."

Jacob said, "No. Keep them for you have received me in
kindness and seeing your face is like seeing the face of the
Divine.
God has given me everything I need."

Afterwards Esau went to Seir while Jacob went and
built a house and booths for his animals
and named the place Sukkot (Shelters).

Vayishlach 33:1-17

Q. How is giving forgiveness different from receiving forgiveness? What
do you do better - give or receive forgiveness?

Tiptoe Through Genesis

Jacob journeyed on {with his families and
possessions) and arrived
in the city of Shechem
in the land of Canaan
safely.

He bought the portion of the field in Shechem
where he pitched his tent.

He set up there an altar
and proclaimed
"God is the God of Israel."

Vayishlach 33:18-20

Q. What purpose does an altar serve? How grateful are you for your
safety?

Leah {and Jacob's} daughter Dinah went out to visit the local
girls and was seen by the Prince of Shechem. He raped her.
But then he fell in love with her and wanted to marry her.

Jacob heard his daughter had been defiled and
remained silent until his sons came from the fields.
The King of Shechem came to him with an offer to intermarry.
And the Prince came and said, "I will do anything to regain
your favor."

When Jacob's sons returned and replied to him
it was with an ulterior motive for their sister had been defiled.
They agreed to intermarriage but only
if all males in Shechem were circumcised.
And it was agreed and done.

On the third day, when the males were in agony
from the circumcision
{two of Dinah's brothers} Simeon and Levi
took up swords and killed every male.
They plundered the city's wealth
and captured the women and children.

Jacob said to Simeon and Levi "You have given me a bad
reputation and the local people might attack us."

They said, "Should he treat our sister like a harlot?"

Vayishlach 34:1-31

Q. When have you had ulterior motives? How would you describe your
reputation?

{After the brothers revenged their sister's rape in Shechem}
God said to Jacob
*Go to BethEl and build an altar to God who appeared to you
when you were fleeing from your brother.*

Jacob gathered his families and servers.
"Get rid of any idols you have and purify
yourself and change your clothes. We are
setting out to BethEl where I will make an
altar to God Who answered me in my time
of trouble
and has been with me on the road I have traveled."

They gave him their idols and he buried them
beneath a tree near Shechem.

Then they set out
and the terror of God was felt in all the cities
so no-one pursued Jacob's sons.

When Jacob arrived in BethEl
he built an altar
for it was there
that God was revealed to him
when he was fleeing his brother.

Vayishlach 35:1-7

Q. How do you feel about idols and God? How do you purify yourself?

Deborah, the wet nurse of Rebecca died and she was buried
in the valley of BethEl under an oak tree.

And God appeared again to Jacob
when he came from Paddan Aram. God
blessed him
Jacob is your name
but Israel
shall also be your name.

God said
I am God Almighty.
Be fruitful and multiply
for a nation
and a congregation of nations
shall descend from you
and kings shall issue from your loins.
The land that I gave to Abraham and to Isaac
I will give to you and your descendants
who follow you.

God went up and left Jacob.
Then Jacob set up a pillar on the place
where God had spoken with him and
offered a libation and poured oil on it.
Jacob named the place where God had spoken to him BethEl
{God's Temple}.

Vayishlach 35:8-15

Q. On earth, is it "your purpose" or "God's purpose for you"? How do
you feel about places of worship?

On the journey away from BethEl Jacob's wife Rachel had a
hard labor
and gave birth - a boy!
And as Rachel's soul
departed in death
she named him
Ben-Oni

"son of my mourning".
But his father
called him Benjamin
"son of strength".

And Rachel died
and was buried on the road to BethEl.
Jacob set up a pillar on her grave
which is there to this day.

Vayishlach 35:16-20

Q. What do you think happens to a soul after the body dies? What
quality best represents you?

{After his beloved Rachel died} Israel {Jacob} traveled on and set up his tent beyond the hill {with Bilbah who had been Rachel's handmaid}.

While Jacob was living there undisturbed
Reuben {his son with his wife Leah}
went there and disturbed
the sleeping arrangements
of Bilbah
his father's concubine.

And Jacob heard about it.

Vayishlach 35:21-22

Q. How do you show respect for the property of others? How involved are you in other people's relationships?

Jacob had twelve sons
when he came
to his father Isaac's home in Mamre
in Hebron
where Abraham had resided.

Isaac lived for 180 years.
He died
and was
old and fulfilled.

His sons Esau and Jacob buried him.

Vayishlach 35:23-29

Q. How do you understand the timing of a person's death? What fulfills you most in life?

In the chronicles
of Esau
(also known as Edom)
he had many
Canaanite wives who bore him children.

Esau left Canaan
with his family, possessions, and flocks for he saw the land
could not handle the property of both brothers and moved to
Seir.
There Esau became the nation of Edom.

Vayishlach 36:1-43

Q. What kind of "space" is good for relationships? How do you define maturity?

Jacob settled
down in the land of his father's sojournings
in the land of Canaan.
These are the chronicles of Jacob.

Joseph
was 17 years old.

Joseph (son of Rachel}
tended sheep
with sons from Bilbah and Zilpah.

Joseph
brought his father
bad reports about them.

Vayashev 37:1-2

Q. How do you feel about gossip? Are you more positive or more
negative when you talk about others?

Now Israel (Jacob) loved Joseph more than all his sons as he was the child of his old age. He made him a fine wool coat of many colors.

When the brothers could see that their
father loved him most they hated him
for it
and could not peaceably speak to him.

Vayashev 37:3-4

Q. How do you measure love? How do you express your hate?

{Joseph was hated by his brothers
because their father Jacob loved him the most.}

Then Joseph dreamt a dream
and when he told it to his brothers
they hated him even more. He said, "Listen.
We were in a field binding sheaves
when behold!
my sheaf arose and stood.
Then behold
your sheaves
gathered around
and bowed down to my sheaf."

His brothers said to him "Do
you mean to reign over us
and dominate us?"

Because of his dreams and words
they hated him
even more.

Vayashev 37:5-8

Q. How do you understand dreaming? Why are words so powerful?

{Joseph's brothers hated him, his colorful coat and his dream
of their sheaves bowing down to his sheaf.}

Joseph dreamt another dream and told
his father and brothers "Behold in this
dream the sun, the moon
and eleven stars were bowing down to me."

His father scolded him, "What is this dream?
Do you want me, your mother and your
brothers to bow down to you on the ground?"

Joseph's brothers hated him
but his father kept the matter in mind.

Vayashev 37:9-11

Q. How does hating impact you? How do you feel about scolding?

Tiptoe Through Genesis

One day when Joseph's brothers were at
pasture his father Israel {Jacob} asked him
to check on his brothers and the flocks and
report back.

Joseph arrived and a stranger
discovered him blundering in the field.

The stranger said, "What
are you looking for?"

Joseph said, "I am searching for my brothers. Perhaps you
can tell me where they are tending sheep?"

The man said, "They already left.
They were planning to go to Dothan."

And Joseph went
and found his brothers in Dothan.

Vayashev 37:12-17

Q. How random are the people we meet in our lives? What is your most
memorable encounter with a stranger?

{Jacob sent his favorite son Joseph to check up on his other
sons tending sheep. Joseph found them}.

And his brothers saw him from afar
{and hated him and his dreams of ruling over them}.

One said to another, "Look! That dreamer is coming! Let us
kill him, throw him into one of the pits and say 'A wild beast
devoured him.' Then we shall see what will become of his
dreams."

Reuben heard these words
and sought to rescue Joseph saying, "Shed no blood! Just
throw him into the pit.
You won't have to lay a hand on him."

(Now Reuben's plan was to come back later
and rescue Joseph.)

And so it was when Joseph came to his brothers
they stripped away his colorful wool tunic
and cast him into an empty waterless pit.

Afterwards they sat down above him
and ate their meal.

Vayashev 37:18-25

Q. How does saving a life save a world? When have you tried to rescue
someone?

{Joseph's brothers had thrown him into an empty pit
and now sat above him eating.}
They looked up.
Behold!
An Arab caravan was coming.

Judah said to his brothers with him
"What will we gain if we kill our brother and
cover up his blood? Let us sell him instead. After
all, he is our brother, our own flesh and blood."

His brothers agreed and they sold Joseph to the Ishmaelite
traders for twenty pieces of silver.

Vayashev 37:25-28

Q. Which of your decisions dramatically changed someone else's life?
How do you understand coincidences?

{As Reuben planned}
he returned to rescue his brother Joseph from the pit.
And behold! Joseph was gone!
Reuben tore his garment in grief
and confronted his younger brothers, "The boy is
gone! How am I going to tell our father about his
beloved Joseph? What will I say happened?"

Thus they took Joseph's colorful coat and
dipped it in the blood of a goat they had
slaughtered. Later the brothers went to their
father Jacob and
said, "We found this. Identify if you wish
this coat, to see if it is your son's."
Jacob recognized it and cried, "My son's coat!
A wild beast must have eaten him.
My Joseph
has been torn to pieces."

Then Jacob ripped his
garment in grief
and mourned for many days.

All of his family tried to console him but
he refused to be comforted. He said "I will
go to my grave mourning my son."

Vayashev 37:29-35

Q. How do you try to console others? What are the most comforting
things someone can do for you?

{Because Joseph's brothers hated him}
Joseph had been sold
to Ishmaelite traders
who
sold him in Egypt
to Potiphar
one of Pharaoh's officers.

{Potiphar was} the Chief of the Guards.

Vayashev 37:36

Q. How do you cope with circumstances beyond your control? When have you felt the most powerless?

It was
{after the brothers sold Joseph to the Ishmaelite caravan}
that Judah left his brothers.

He went with a man to Abdullam
and met there
and wed Shua and they
had three sons.

Judah took a wife for Er, his firstborn. Her name was Tamar.
But Er, the firstborn, was evil in God's eyes and God caused
him to die.

Vayashev 38:1-7

Q. In God's eyes, has evil changed over time? How important to you is
the "cause of death"?

{Judah took Tamar as a wife for his firstborn son Er. But Er was evil and God caused him to die.}

Then Judah said to his second born Onan "Marry your brother's wife and fulfill your {levirate marriage}. You will then have children to keep your brother's name alive."

But Onan knew
the children would not be known as his; so whenever he would consort with his brother's wife he would let his seed be wasted so as not to provide offspring for his brother. What he did was evil in God's eyes
and God also caused him to die.

Judah said to his daughter-in-law Tamar "Remain a widow in your father's house until my {youngest} son Shelah grows up." He was putting her off for he was concerned his {remaining} son would die like his brothers.
And Tamar left
to go live in her father's house.

Vayashev 38:8-11

Q. How valid is Judah's concern? How do you keep someone's memory alive?

Later, after Judah's wife passed away, he
sought consolation by going to Timna to shear
sheep. When Tamar
{the widow of Judah's two deceased sons}
heard her father-in-law was coming {to Timna}
she took off her widow's garb and veiled herself.

Disguised now as a prostitute
Tamar sat by the crossroad to Timna; for she had
seen that {Judah's third son} Shelah had grown
and she had not been
given to him as a wife
{as Judah promised}.

When Judah saw her covered face he
approached her as a prostitute for he did not know she was
his daughter-in-law. She said "What will you give me?"

He said, "I will send you a kid from my goat flock."

She said, "As long as you give me some security until it
arrives. Give me your signet ring, your wrap and the staff in
your hand."
And he agreed and she conceived by him. Then she arose,
left, removed her veil and put back on her widow's garb.

Vayashev 38:12-19

Q. To what lengths will you go to get what you want? What gives you a
sense of security?

As Judah promised he sent his friend to Timna with a goat to
pay his prostitute. But his friend did not find her. Judah said to
him, "Let her keep
{my signet ring, wrap and walking stick}
lest we become a laughingstock?"

It was about three months later
when Judah was told, "Your daughter-in-law Tamar
acted like a prostitute
and now has conceived a child through her looseness."

Judah said, "Take her out and let her be burned."

As she was taken out
Tamar sent word to her father-in-law
"These are the items
which belong to the man with whom I conceived. Identify, if
you please, who is the owner of this this signet ring, this wrap
and this staff?"

Judah immediately recognized them. "She is more
righteous than I because I did not give her
{as I promised} to Shelah, my younger son.
And he was not intimate with her anymore.

Vayashev 38:20-26

Q. How much effort do you put into proving people wrong? How willing
are you to admit when you are wrong?

{Tamar conceived from Judah.}

When she gave birth
behold!
There were twins in her womb
and as she gave birth
one put out a hand
and the midwife took a crimson thread
and tied it on his hand saying
"This one came
out first!"
And as he drew back his hand
behold!
His brother emerged
and the midwife said
"With what strength
you asserted yourself!"
And she called his name Perez.

Afterwards his brother on whose hand
was the crimson thread
came out.
She called his name Zerah.

Vayashev 38:27-30

Q. What kind of strength do you need to assert yourself? With whom do
you have the hardest time asserting yourself?

{After being sold by his brothers to a passing caravan}
Joseph was brought down to Egypt.
Potiphar
Pharaoh's Captain of the Guards
purchased him
from the Ishmaelites who had brought him there.

In Egypt
God was with Joseph
and he became a successful man
working at his master {Potiphar's} own house.

Potiphar perceived
that God was with Joseph
and appointed him
over his entire household
giving him responsibility for everything he owned.

Afterwards
God blessed
the Egyptian's house and fields
on Joseph's account.

Vayashev 39:1-5

**Q. Can you perceive when "God is with" someone? Does God still bless
one person on account of another?**

{In Egypt}
Joseph gained favor with his master Potiphar
and before long
he was appointed as his personal servant
in charge of his household and everything he owned.
Potiphar left everything in Joseph's hands
except the food he ate.

{Now} Joseph was well built and handsome
and Potiphar's wife cast her eyes upon him
saying, "Lay with me."

But Joseph adamantly refused "How could I do this great evil
to my master and sin against God?"

Day after day she coaxed Joseph
but he would not go to her.

Vayashev 39:6-10

Q. What does Joseph value? Why are boundaries necessary in
relationships?

Tiptoe Through Genesis

{Day after day Potiphar's wife
coaxed her husband's servant Joseph
to lay with her but he would not go near her.}

One such day
when Joseph came to the house to work
and no staff was inside
she grabbed him by his garment and pleaded
but he tore away
leaving the garment in her hand.
When she saw
she had Joseph's cloak, she cried out, "Look!
The Hebrew slave attacked me and when I screamed
he left his garment and ran outside."

When
Potiphar heard his wife's words, his anger flared against
Joseph. He had him arrested and thrown into the dungeon
with the rest of Pharaoh's prisoners.

Vayashev 39:11-20

Q. Have you ever lied to get back at someone? How do you respond
when someone sets a boundary with you?

{Trusted servant Joseph was thrown into
the royal dungeon by his master Potiphar
after his wife falsely accused Joseph of attacking her.}

In jail
God was with Joseph
and endowed him with charisma.

And the prison warden favored him
and put Joseph in charge of the inmates.

Joseph took care of everything that had to be done.
God was with Joseph
granting him success in all that he did.

Vayashev 39:21-23

Q. What is the relationship between God, personal responsibility and
success? With what are you endowed?

{With God's help
the warden of the royal jail favored Joseph
and appointed him to oversee all the other prisoners.}

It came to happen that the chief wine
steward and the chief baker were
arrested and put in jail for offending their
master Pharaoh of Egypt. The royal
warden put them in Joseph's personal
custody.

One morning they were downcast and
Joseph asked about their worry.

They said, "We both had dreams
but we have no interpreter."

Joseph said
"Do not {dream} interpretations belong to God?
Tell me
if you please."

Vayashev 40:1-8

Q. How do dream interpretations "belong to God"? Do you ask people
about their true feelings?

{In Pharaoh's dungeon, Joseph listened to the dreams of the
two prisoners in his custody.}

The wine steward said, "There was
a grapevine with three branches ripening into clusters of
grapes and I pressed the grapes into Pharaoh's cup to drink."

And Joseph said
"Pharaoh will restore you to your post in three days.
Do me a kindness.
Speak to Pharaoh of my innocence."

Then the baker said
"There were three wicker baskets filled with
baked goods and birds were eating from it."

And Joseph said
"In three days, the Pharaoh will hang you."

It was on the third day
at Pharaoh's birthday feast for his servants that Pharaoh
restored the wine steward to his post and hung the baker just
as Joseph predicted.
But the wine steward did not remember
Joseph to the Pharaoh. He forgot all
about him.

Vayashev 40:9-23

Q. How forgetful are you? What effort is required to "remember"?

It came to pass
after two years
that Pharaoh had a dream. He was standing near the river
when seven robust cows emerged and grazed. Behold!

Seven gaunt cows emerged
and ate the healthy cows.

Pharaoh woke up
then fell back asleep.
He had a second dream
and dreamt
of seven healthy ears of grain sprouts
on a single stalk.
And then
seven thin ears of grain appeared and
swallowed up the seven full sprouted ones!
Pharaoh awoke and behold!

It had been a dream.

In the morning Pharaoh was very upset and sent for all his
wise men to interpret his dreams. But no one could provide
him
a satisfactory interpretation.

Miketz 41:1-8

Q. What is wisdom? In what ways are you wise?

{Pharaoh was very upset that no one could satisfactorily
interpret his two dreams.} It was then
the Pharaoh's wine steward spoke up
"I regret
to bring up my transgressions to Pharaoh but
when I was sent to prison with the royal baker
we both had dreams.
The Hebrew prisoner who oversaw the other prisoners
interpreted our dreams and things worked out just as he said
they would. I was given back my position and the royal baker
was hanged."

And Pharaoh sent messengers
and had Joseph summoned.

Miketz 41:9-14

Q. How is revealing a transgression courage? What is the most
courageous thing you have ever done?

{Pharaoh summoned the dream interpreting Hebrew prisoner who oversaw the other prisoners.}

And Pharaoh's servers rushed Joseph
from jail shaved him, bathed him, then
dressed him in different clothes.
Afterwards Joseph was presented to Pharaoh.
Pharaoh said, "I hear you interpret dreams."

Joseph said, "That is beyond me. It is God Who will provide
an answer regarding Pharaoh's welfare."

Then Pharaoh told Joseph his dreams.
"In my dream I was standing on the bank of the
Nile {river}. Suddenly, seven fat handsome cows
emerged and grazed in the marsh. Then, just as
suddenly, seven other cows emerged but these
were badly formed and emaciated. The
emaciated ones proceeded
to eat the healthy cows but afterwards
they looked just as bad. Then I dreamt
of seven full, good ears of grain growing on a single stalk.
Suddenly seven other ears grew behind them but they were
shriveled, thin and scorched by the east (desert) wind. The
thin ears swallowed up the seven good ears."

Joseph said
"It is but one dream
stating what God is about to do."

Miketz 41:14-25

Q. How does Joseph know? How do clothes affect perceptions?

{Joseph, the Hebrew prisoner who oversaw the other
prisoners, listened to Pharaoh's two dreams. He said, "It is
but one dream with a single meaning. God has shown
Pharaoh
what God is about to do.}

There will be seven years of abundant harvest
followed by seven years of severe famine.

Now let Pharaoh seek out a wise discerning Overseer to
store and safeguard the grain during abundant years and
distribute it during the famine so Egypt shall not perish. That
you dreamt it twice means God has set the process in motion,
hastening it."

Appearing to be an excellent plan
Pharaoh reflected to his advisors "Could we find another man
like him with his Spirit of God?"

Then Pharaoh told Joseph, "Since God informed you of this,
there is no-one more discerning or wiser. You shall be the
Overseer over the entire land of Egypt and by your command
shall all my peoples be sustained. Only by my throne shall I
outrank you."

Pharaoh then took the royal ring off his own hand and gave it
to Joseph.

Miketz 41:26-42

Q. What does it mean for the Pharaoh to acknowledge God and
Joseph? When has your life changed in an instant?

Tiptoe Through Genesis

{The Hebrew inmate who oversaw the other prisoners
Joseph
interpreted Pharaoh's dreams.
Pharoah made him Egypt's
Overseer of Grain and
gave him his own royal ring.}
Then he had Joseph
dressed in the finest linen and a gold
chain was put around his neck.

Pharaoh had him ride in the second
royal chariot with those going ahead of
him announcing "The Viceroy!"

Joseph was thus given
authority over all of Egypt.

Pharaoh gave Joseph
the name Tzaphnath Paaneach.
He gave him
Asenath, daughter of a priest.

When he stood before Pharaoh
Joseph was 30 years old.

Miketz 41:43-46

Q. Is Joseph prepared for this kind of power? How do you like to be
acknowledged?

{After Pharaoh announced Joseph as the royal Overseer of grain and Viceroy over all Egypt} Joseph left from Pharaoh's presence and passed through the entire land of Egypt assessing supplies.

During the seven years of surplus
when the land produced loads of grain
Joseph had them collect it
and placed the food in cities.

Joseph accumulated so much grain it was like the sands of the sea too numerous to count.

Miketz 41:47-49

Q. What do you accumulate? What situation in your life needs assessing?

{Pharaoh proclaimed the former prisoner Joseph Egypt's
Viceroy and Overseer of grain and gave him a wife.}

Joseph had two sons before the famine years came.
They were born to Asenath
daughter of a priest of On.

Joseph named the first one
Manasseh
for "God has made me forget all my troubles." His second one
he named Ephraim
for "God has made me fruitful
in the land of my suffering."

Miketz 41:50-52

Q. Do you try to find "good" amidst suffering? What helps you forget your troubles?

{In all of Egypt}
the seven years of abundance
came to an end
and the seven years of famine began
just
as Joseph had predicted.

And the famine spread throughout
all the lands.
Only in Egypt was there bread.

Later all of Egypt hungered too.
{And} the people called out to Pharaoh for bread.

Pharaoh announced, "Go to Joseph.
Do whatever he tells you."

Joseph opened the storehouses
and rationed out the supplies.
But the famine grew more severe
and people came from all over to Egypt
to obtain rations from Joseph.

Miketz 41:53-57

Q. What makes a good leader? What do you ration?

{Famine spread throughout the lands in Canaan
where Jacob lived with his eleven sons.}

Jacob learned that there were provisions in Egypt.
He said to his sons
"Go to Egypt and buy food
so that we may live
and not die."

So Joseph's ten brothers
went down
like many others
to buy grain in Egypt.

But Jacob did not send {his youngest son} Benjamin with his
brothers "Lest something happen to him."

Miketz 42:1-4

**Q. How do you protect those you love? With whom do you feel the most
protective?**

{Jacob's} sons went to Egypt
like many others for famine
was in the land of Canaan.

Now Joseph was the Overseer and the only one who rationed
out the grain for all the people.

When Joseph's brothers arrived
they bowed down
before him
with their faces to the ground.

Miketz 42:5-6

Q. Over whom do you have power? Who has power over you?

Joseph
{Pharaoh's Overseer of grain}
recognized
his brothers bowing to him
as soon as he saw them
but he acted like a stranger.
He spoke to them harshly.
"Where are you from?"

The brothers did not recognize their brother. They said "From
the land of Canaan to buy food."

Joseph remembered
the dreams he had
about his brothers {bowing down to him}. He said, "No. You
are spies. You came to see the nakedness of the land."

"No, my lord!" the {brothers} replied. "We are
your servants who came only to buy food. We
are all sons of the same man. We are
honorable men. We would never think of being
spies."

"No," Joseph retorted. "You have come
to see the nakedness of the land."

Miketz 42:7-12

Q. What do you do with the power you have? Have you ever been
falsely accused?

{Unbeknownst to the ten brothers, they stood before Joseph,
their brother who was now Egypt's Overseer of grain. They
came only to buy food but
the Overseer accused them of being spies.}
They said
"We are twelve brothers. We are the sons
of one man who is in Canaan.
Right now the youngest brother is with our father and one
brother is gone."

Joseph said, "It is as I say. You are spies. And there is only
one way to convince me otherwise.
I shall keep one brother here while the rest of you go and
bring supplies to your hungry families.

Do not return without your youngest brother
for it is by this act
that the truth will be known."

Then Joseph had them
thrown in jail for three days.

Miketz 42:13-17

Q. How is truth known? Have you ever falsely accused someone?

Tiptoe Through Genesis

{{Egypt's Overseer Joseph recognized his ten
brothers coming to buy food but they did not
recognize him. And he jailed them for being
spies.}
On the third day, Joseph said to them, "If you do as I say
you will live
for I fear God.
If you are truthful people
leave one brother with me
and go take supplies to your hungry families.
Return later with your youngest brother {to
receive more supplies} so that you may live."

They agreed {to do this}. Then one brother
said to another
"Indeed we are guilty of ignoring Joseph's sufferings
when he pleaded with us not to sell him.
This is the cause of all of our misfortune."

Then the eldest, {brother} Reuben said, "Did I not tell you to
not sin against the boy? This is a Divine accounting."

Now since
the brothers used an interpreter
they did not know that Joseph understood.
And Joseph
had to turn away and leave the room
to weep.

Miketz 42:18-24

**Q. Do you believe in a Divine accounting? How do understand your
misfortunes?**

{When Joseph heard the regret of his brothers
for having sold him, he rushed from the room to weep.}
When he regained his composure
he returned to his brothers
then
jailed Simeon before their very eyes.

{Later}
Joseph told his server
that when the sack of each brother
was filled with {their purchased} grain
to return
their payment.

So the brothers loaded their donkeys with the food they
purchased and departed. Later, when stopping for the
night, one brother opened his sack to feed his donkey
and saw
behold!
His money was in the mouth of his sack!
He told his brothers, "That is the exact money I used to buy
my grain. It has been returned to my sack." The brothers
trembled with each other "What is this
that
God has done to us?"

MiKetz 42:25-28

Q. What makes you tremble? How do you regain your composure?

After their journey, the brothers came
to their father Jacob in Canaan
and they told him all that had happened.
They said "The man who was the lord
{Overseer} of the land spoke harshly and
accused us of spying.
We said, 'We are honorable men. We have
never been spies. We are twelve brothers,
all from the same father. One of us is lost
and the youngest is with our father in
Canaan.'

{Then} the man who was the lord of the land
said to us 'I have a way of knowing if you are
truthful. Leave one of your brothers with me
and go take food to your hungry families.
When you return for more food
bring your youngest to me
{then} I will know you are not spies
but honorable people.
Then I will restore your brother to you
and you will be free to do business in the land'."

All the brothers then began to empty their sacks and behold!
Every man's exact grain payment!
When they and their father saw the bundles of
money they were terrified.

Miketz 42:29-35

Q. How are you honorable? How does it feel to speak harshly?

{When Jacob heard how Egypt's Overseer of
grain had jailed his son Simeon for spying and
to not return to Egypt for food without his youngest son}
Jacob said to his sons, "You have bereaved me.
Joseph is gone. Simeon is gone and now
you would take Benjamin. Upon me has
everything fallen!"

Reuben said to his father
"You may slay my two sons
if I fail to bring him back to you.
Put him in my care and I will return him to you."

Jacob said
"My son shall not go down with you
for his brother is dead and
he alone is left {from my beloved wife Rachel}.
Should disaster strike him along the way
you will bring {me}
in my old age
down to the grave in misery!"

Miketz 42:36-38

Q. Are you able to avoid disaster? When have you made extreme
promises?"

{The only way Jacob's ten sons were to return
to Egypt's Overseer for food rations was to
bring their youngest brother Benjamin.}

The famine was very severe {in Canaan}.
And when they had used up all their
supplies Judah said to his father Israel
{Jacob} "Let's live and not all die. I myself
will take responsibility for Benjamin and I
will have sinned for all time if I don't bring
him back."

Israel {Jacob} said, "Why did you
do such a terrible thing to me
telling the man you had another brother?"

They said, "The man kept asking about us also
our family. How were we to know
he would make us bring him?"

And their father said to them, "If it must be so,
so be it. Take him our land's finest spices and
nuts as tributes. And take enough money to pay
double for the new grain. Also return the
payment for the grain that reappeared. Maybe it
was an oversight. And may God All-Sufficing
grant you mercy before this man so that
Benjamin and Simeon may be released.
As I have been bereaved so am I to be bereaved."
Thereafter the men took everything and left.

Miketz 43:1-15

Q. What does acceptance require? How much of life do you control?

{The famine grew so severe
Jacob let all his remaining sons return
to Egypt's Overseer for food rations.} And the
brothers stood before him {but did not know he
was Joseph}.

When Joseph saw {his younger brother} Benjamin
he said to his household supervisor
"Bring these men into the palace and
prepare a feast.
These men shall dine with me at noon."

{Thus} the brothers were brought to Joseph's palace. Then
they realized it was his personal home! And they were
terrified.

They said {to each other}, "We are brought here because of
the money we found in our sacks.
It's going to be used against us to fabricate a crime
and convict us
and make slaves of us and our donkeys."

Miketz 43:15-18

Q. How often do you jump to negative conclusions? When do you feel
intimidated?

At the entrance of the personal home of
Egypt's royal Overseer of grain the brothers
went directly to his household supervisor. The
brothers said

"If you please sir, we came here
{before} to buy food and paid our
money for it. But later when we stopped
for the night we opened our sacks
and each of us found our exact payment.

We brought that money back with us
and we will pay
double to buy more grain for we have no idea
who put the money in our sacks."

The supervisor {of Joseph's household} said "Peace be with
you, fear not. Your God and the God of your father has given
you a hidden treasure in your sack. Your payment reached
me."

And he brought {their brother} Simeon out to them and
together the brothers
were brought inside Joseph's palace.
He gave them all water to wash their
feet and feed for their animals.

Miketz 43:19-24

Q. How honest are you? When do you feel most at peace?

{Inside Joseph's personal palace} the brothers displayed the delicacies they brought for Egypt's Overseer for they had heard they would be dining with him at noon.

When Joseph arrived home
they presented their gifts
and bowed down to the ground.
He inquired about their welfare then said
"Is your aged father in peace and alive?"

They said, "He is at peace and still alive."
And they bowed completely down to the ground.

Joseph lifted his eyes and saw
his brother Benjamin, his mother {Rachel's} son. He said, "Is this your younger brother whom you spoke about? My son, may God be gracious to you." Then
so stirred with feelings
Joseph rushed to another room to weep.

Afterwards Joseph washed his face and went out. He fortified himself and said, "Serve the meal."

Miketz 43:25-31

Q. How do you fortify yourself? How does crying feel to you?

For lunch in his home Joseph {Egypt's
Viceroy and Overseer} was served by
himself and {the brothers} by
themselves.

The Egyptians also ate separately
as they did not eat with the Hebrews
since this was taboo for Egyptians.

When the brothers were seated before {Joseph's table} they
were seated from oldest to the youngest. {They did not know
the Overseer was their brother.}

The brothers looked at each other in amazement
as Joseph sent large portions of food
from his table to theirs
and Benjamin received five extra portions.

They feasted and drank and became intoxicated.

Miketz 43:32-34

Q. What is your idea of a feast? What occasion truly amazed you?

{While Joseph's brothers
were feasting and drinking}
Egypt's Overseer Joseph gave his household
supervisor special instructions for the brothers. "Fill
their packs with as much food as they can carry.
Then put the money they paid back in their sacks and
put my special silver goblet in the youngest one's sack."
And the server did.

In the first morning light
the brothers left and had not gone far before
Joseph said to his household supervisor
"Set out and pursue those men.
When you catch them
say to them
'Why did you repay good for evil?
This {goblet} is the one from which my master drinks
and he uses it for divination.
You have done a terrible thing'."

Miketz 44:1-5

Q. Have you ever repaid good with evil? In what ways do you make
things hard for others?

Tiptoe Through Genesis

{Egypt's Overseer Joseph sent his household supervisor to
accuse his brothers of stealing his silver goblet.} After the
servant told them this
the brothers said
"Why my lord would you say such things?
It would be sacrilegious!
Look. We brought back the money we found in our sacks.
How could we steal silver or gold from your master's
house? If anyone has it in his possession
he shall die
and you can take the rest of us as slaves."

The {Overseer's} household supervisor said
"It should be as you say
but only the one
with whom it is found
will become a slave
and the rest of you shall be exonerated."

Each of the brothers quickly
lowered his pack to the ground and opened it.
And he inspected each sack
eldest to youngest.
And the goblet was found
in {youngest brother} Benjamin's sack.

Miketz 44:6-12

Q. What is sacrilegious to you? When have you set someone up to fail?

{The royal Overseer's goblet was found in the sack of
Benjamin, their father's favorite son}
and the brothers tore their clothes in grief. Then each of them
reloaded their donkeys and returned to the city.

When Judah and his brothers
arrived back at Joseph's palace
{the Overseer} was still there.
They fell upon the ground before him.
Joseph said to them, "What did you think
you were doing {stealing my goblet}? Did
you not know that a man like me practices
divination?"

So Judah said, "What can we say
to my lord?
How can we speak? How can we justify ourselves?
God has uncovered the sins of your servants.
Let us be your slaves
—we and on who it was found."

Miketz 44:13-16

Q. How loyal are you to your family? What do justify?

{Brother Judah said to the Overseer, "Let us be your slaves –
we and on whom the divining goblet was found."}

The Overseer said, "That would be sacrilegious for me.
Only he who possessed it shall be my slave.
The rest of you go in peace to your father."

Judah walked up to him, "Please, my lord
let me speak a word
and be not angry even though you are like Pharaoh.
You asked {of our family}.
We said, 'We have an old father and our youngest brother is
the child of his old age. His brother is dead so he is the only
{son of Rachel} left.' He loves him.
So if I go to our father
his soul is so bound up with Benjamin
that when he sees he is not there - he will die.
I promised
to return him. Let me be your slave instead of him
for I cannot bear
to see my father suffer such misery."

Joseph now could no longer restrain his feelings
and asked all the servers to leave.
Thus Joseph
was alone when he made himself
known to his brothers.

Miketz 44:17-45:1

Q. To whom do you reveal your true self? How do you try to minimize
the suffering of others?

{Egypt's Overseer Joseph was alone
when he made himself known to his brothers.}
And Joseph wept so loudly
it could be heard throughout the palace and Egypt.
He said, "I am Joseph.
Is my father still alive?"

But his brothers - shocked and dismayed
could not answer.

Joseph said, "Please come close to me." And they came
close. He said, "It is me you sold into Egypt.
Now do not be distressed or reproach yourselves
for it was God Who sent me ahead to
provide for survival in the land
and to sustain you
for a momentous deliverance.
It was not you who sent me but God.
Now hurry, go say to my father
'Joseph said, 'God has made me master over all of Egypt.
You will live in Goshen and be near to me. I will provide for
you and all your families and livestock so
during the next five years of famine you and your household
will not become destitute'.' Hurry, go and bring father here."

{Then} Joseph fell weeping upon Benjamin's neck
and kissed all his brothers and wept
and after that
the brothers talked with him.

Vayigash 45:2-15

Q. Does everything come from God? Do you look for meaning in what
happens to you in life?

The news of Joseph's brothers was heard throughout the palace and it was pleasing in the eyes of Pharaoh. He told Joseph, "Tell your brothers, 'Bring your father and his household to
me. I will give you the best of Egypt's land.' {And also} take some wagons {to transport} your small
children, your wives and your father.
Take not pity on your belongings
for the best of all the land of Egypt is yours."

The sons of Israel {Jacob} did so and Joseph gave them wagons by Pharaoh's word and provisions for the journey. He gave each a change of clothes, but to {brother} Benjamin he gave three hundred pieces of
silver and five changes of clothing.
For his father
he gave twenty donkeys with Egypt's best delicacies and food supplies for his journey. {As they left}
Joseph said to his brothers
"Do not have any agitation on the way."

Vayigash 45:16-24

Q. How generous are you with family? What do you take pity on?

When the sons of Israel reached the land of Canaan and
come to their father, they said "Joseph is still alive and he is
the Viceroy of Egypt and Overseer of grain."

Jacob's heart stopped
as he could not believe it.
But
then
Jacob looked
and saw all the royal wagons for transporting
and his spirit was revived. He said
"It's too much!
My son Joseph still lives!
I must go
and see him before I die."

Vayigash 45:25-28

Q. What revives your spirit? What has been the best surprise of your life?

So Israel {Jacob} set out with all that he had
{to Egypt where his long thought dead son
Joseph was the royal Overseer}.

In Beer Sheba, Jacob built an altar
and made offerings to God of his father Isaac.

Later God said to Israel in a vision of the night
Jacob. Jacob.

And he said, *"Here I am."*

And God said *I am the Omnipotent God of your father. Have
no fear of going to Egypt. For it is there*

*I shall establish you as a great nation.
I shall descend with you into Egypt
and I shall also surely bring you up
and Joseph shall place his hand on your eyes.*

Vayigash 46:1-4

Q. What does Omnipotent God mean to you? Who gives you hope?

{Because Jacob's son Joseph
was now Egypt's Overseer
Pharaoh sent wagons for transporting him.}
Jacob used these wagons and went
with his children and wives, livestock
and all their wealth they had gained in Canaan.

And they came to Egypt.
These are the names of the Israelites:
Jacob and his sons
Reuben, Simeon, Levi
Judah, Issachar, Zebulun
Gad, Asher, Asher
Benjamin, Dan, Naphtali
and all their descendants.

All the people of Jacob's household who
came to Egypt totaled seventy.

Vayigash 46:5-27

Q. What bonds keep a family together? When has life taken you on an unexpected journey?

{All of Jacob's household was moved to Egypt in Pharaoh's
wagons for his son Joseph had become Egypt's Viceroy and
Overseer.}

Jacob sent his son Judah
ahead to Joseph
to prepare for their arrival in Goshen.

Joseph
{personally} harnessed his own chariot
and went up to meet his father Israel {Jacob} in Goshen.

Joseph came to his father and threw
himself upon his shoulders and wept
there.

Israel {Jacob} said
"I can die now because I have seen your face
and know you are alive."

Vayigash 46:28-30

Q. How do you show respect to your parents? When have you had a
"happy ending"?

Joseph said to his brothers
"I will go to Pharaoh and say you are shepherds
and that you have brought your livestock.
So when Pharaoh
summons you and asks your occupation say
'shepherds'
since they are taboo in Egypt."

Then from among his brothers Joseph selected
five and presented them to Pharaoh.

Pharaoh asked, "What is your occupation?"

They said, "We are shepherds like our fathers before us and
have come here to stay because there is no land for grazing
and the famine is severe in Canaan."

Pharaoh said to Joseph, "Your father and
brothers have come to you. Settle them in the best areas
in Goshen. If you have capable men appoint them over
my livestock."

Vayigash 46:31-47:6

Q. What is your process for preparing for important conversations?
How consciously do you introduce someone?

Tiptoe Through Genesis

Joseph presented his father to Pharaoh.

Jacob blessed Pharaoh.

Pharaoh said, "How old are you?"

Jacob replied, "My journey through life has lasted 130 years.
The days of my life have been few and hard
and I am not yet as old as my forefathers." With that Jacob
blessed Pharaoh and left his presence.

Joseph settled his father and brothers as Pharaoh decreed in
the best land of Egypt.

{Throughout the famine} Joseph sustained his father and his
brothers and all his father's households.

Vayigash 47:7-12

Q. In what ways, do you sustain others? In what ways do others sustain
you?

{Now} there was no bread
in the entire area
of Egypt and Canaan.
And the people
were weak with hunger.

{Egypt's Overseer of grain} Joseph collected
all
the people's money
in payment for their food {rations}
and brought the money
to Pharaoh's palace.

Vayigash 47:13-14

Q. What role has money played in your life? How does hunger affect you?

As the famine continued in Egypt and Canaan
the people had no money and came to {Overseer} Joseph.
"Give us bread," they cried. "Why
should we die in your presence
because we have no money?"

Joseph said, "Bring your livestock
and I will provide for you."

Thus they brought their livestock to Joseph and
Joseph gave them food
for their horses, sheep, cattle and donkeys. Thus he provided
for {them and} their livestock throughout that year.

Vayigash 47:15-17

Q. How does it feel to provide for others? How willing are you to ask for what you need?

That year {of the long famine} ended
and the people returned
{to Joseph, Egypt's Overseer of grain}.
"We hold nothing back from you my lord.
We have no livestock and no money.
We have nothing left but our dried up bodies
and our land. Why should we
die before your very eyes
us and our land?
Buy our bodies and our land in exchange for
seed grain so that we may live and not die
and the land shall not become desolate."

Thus
Joseph acquired all the land of Egypt for Pharaoh.
Every Egyptian sold his field
for the famine overwhelmed them all. Only the priest's land
did Joseph not buy for Pharaoh gave them a stipend.
And Joseph announced
"Today I have purchased your bodies and your
lands for Pharaoh. Here is seed grain to plant.
When it produces you will give a fifth to Pharaoh
and the rest shall be yours."

They said, "You have saved our lives."

Vayigash 47:18-26

Q. How does Joseph preserve their dignity? Do you preserve the
dignity of others?

Tiptoe Through Genesis

Israel {Jacob} and his families
settled in the land of Egypt in Goshen.

They acquired property and
were fruitful and multiplied greatly.

Jacob made Egypt his home for seventeen years.
He lived to be a 147 and
when he realized he was going to die
Israel {Jacob} beckoned his son Joseph. He said
"If you want to do me a kindness
{promise to} act towards me
in truth and kindness and do not bury me in Egypt.
Let me lie with my fathers.
Carry me out of Egypt
and bury me in their grave."

Joseph made this oath to him
and from his bed
Israel bowed.

Vayigash 47:27-31

Q. Does your mortality affect the way you live? How do you express your kindness?

It came to pass that Jacob fell ill and
Joseph heard and went to his dying father.

He took his two sons
Manasseh and Ephraim with him.

Summoning his strength Jacob sat up in bed for Joseph. He
said, "God Almighty
once appeared to me in Canaan.
God blessed me and said to me
*I will make you fruitful and numerous
and have you
give rise to an assembly of nations.
I will give this land to you and your descendants
as an eternal possession.*
{So} the two sons born in Egypt
Ephraim and Manasseh
shall be considered {for inheritance} as mine.
Any children afterwards
shall be considered
yours and inherit only through older brothers."

Vayechi 48:1-6

Q. What is your inheritance? What requires your strength?

Tiptoe Through Genesis

{Israel (Jacob) was dying
but summoned the strength to sit up in bed to
talk to Joseph.} He said, "Your mother Rachel
died on the road in Canaan and I buried her
there along the road to Ephrath (Bethlehem)."
Just then
Jacob saw Joseph's sons.
"Who are these?"

Joseph said, "These are the two sons
God has given me here."

Jacob said, "If you bring them to me
I will give them a blessing."

Israel could not see and when they came near he kissed
them and hugged them. Israel said to Joseph "I dared not
accept the thought that I would see your face and here God
has shown me even your offspring."

Vayechi 48:7-11

Q. Do you give God credit for the good in your life? How do you feel
about physical affection?

Israel {Jacob} sat
up in bed as Joseph positioned his two sons
{for his father's blessings} placing elder Ephraim to his right
and younger Manasseh to his left. But Israel
extended his right hand and laid it on
Ephraim's head
and his left hand on Manasseh's head.
He deliberately crossed his
hands for Manasseh was firstborn.

Jacob gave Joseph a blessing. "God before whom my fathers
Abraham and Isaac walked
is the God Who has been my shepherd
from as far back as I can remember
until this day.
The angel
who redeems me from all evil
bless the lads
and let them carry my name
along with the names of my fathers
Abraham and Isaac.
May they increase in the land
like fish in the seas."

Vayechi 48:12-16

Q. How long has God been with you? What do you do deliberately?

Tiptoe Through Genesis

{Joseph saw his father Jacob crossing his
hands over his sons to bless them and it
displeased him.} He tried to lift his father's
hand
from {younger} Ephraims's head to
{elder} Manasseh's head. He said
"Father, that's not how it's done here.

The firstborn gets the blessing with your right hand."

His father refused and said, "I know my son.
The older one will become a people
and he will become great
yet
his younger brother shall
become even greater and his descendants will
become a famous nation."

On that day {Jacob} blessed them. He said
"In time to come Israel will use you as a blessing.
They will say 'May God make you
like Ephraim and Manasseh'."
He deliberately
put Ephraim before Manasseh.

Vayechi 48:17-20

**Q. Why is it important to bless our children? How do you handle it when
others do something differently than you would?**

Israel {Jacob} said to his son Joseph
"Behold. I am about to die.
God will be with you and
will bring you back to the land of our ancestors. I give you
Shechem {which is} one land more than your brothers."

{Later} Jacob called for his sons and said
"Assemble yourselves and
I will tell you
what will befall each of you
in the end of days.
Keep together
and listen
O sons of Jacob.
Listen to Israel your father."

Vayechi 48:21- 49:2

Q. How do you understand the "end of days"? What does "keep together" mean to you?

{Jacob is dying and is surrounded by his twelve sons. He tells them what will befall them in the end of days. He said, "Listen to Israel, your father.}

Reuben
you are my firstborn
my strength and the beginning of my manhood
foremost in rank and foremost in power.

But like running water you rushed
recklessly. You cannot be
foremost because you disturbed
my bed and desecrated it."

Vayechi 49:3-4

Q. When have you rushed recklessly? How does your birth order affect you?

{Jacob is dying and is surrounded by his twelve sons. He tells them what will befall them in the end of days. He said, "Listen to Israel, your father.}

Shimeon and Levi
are brothers
who used stolen weapons
for gain.
Let not my soul nor my honor
be joined with their plots
for in their rage
they murdered
and
lamed an ox
with intent.
Cursed is their intense rage
and harsh is their wrath.

I will divide them within Jacob
and scatter them in Israel."

Vayechi 49:5-7

Q. What have you done in rage? How do you preserve your honor?

{Jacob is dying and is surrounded by his twelve sons. He tells them what will befall them in the end of days. He said, "Listen to Israel, your father.}

Judah
you are the one. To you
will your brothers acknowledge.
Your hand will be at the neck of your enemy.
The sons of your father will bow to you.

A cub of a lion is Judah. From prey,
you have elevated yourself. He
crouches
laying down like a lion, an awesome lion.
Who dare rouse him?

The scepter {royal emblem) will not depart from Judah
nor the writing of law from among his descendants
until Shiloh arrives and his
will be an assembly of nations.
He will tie his donkey to the vine {and} to the
vine branch his donkey's foal. He even launders
his garments in wine; his robe with the blood of grapes.
His eyes sparkle from wine
his teeth whitened from milk."

Vayechi 49:8-12

Q. From what, do you try to elevate yourself? How do you envision Shiloh's assembly of nations?

{Jacob is dying and is surrounded by his twelve sons. He tells them what will befall them in the end of days. He said, "Listen to Israel, your father.}

Zebulun
will dwell at a bay of seas.
He will become a harbor for ships.
His border shall reach Sidon.

Yissakhar
is a strong-boned donkey.
He rests between the
boundaries.
He saw the good tranquility of the pleasant land
yet he bent his shoulder to the burden
and became the one {to pay} the service levy."

Vayechi 49:13-15

Q. How do you approach your burdens? Where is your safe harbor?

Tiptoe Through Genesis

{Jacob is dying and is surrounded by his twelve sons. He tells them what will befall them in the end of days. He said, "Listen to Israel, your father.}

Dan
will exact justice for his people
equal to the unique one among the tribes of Israel.

Dan will become a serpent on the highway
a viper, by the path, which
bites the heel of a horse
so that the rider falls backward.
For your salvation
do I long
O God.

Gad
a troop
shall troop forth
and it will
troop back
on its footsteps."

Vayechi 49:16-19

Q. What kind of salvation do you long for from God? How does "leaving and returning" change you?

{Jacob is dying and is surrounded by his twelve sons. He tells them what will befall them in the end of days. He said, "Listen to Israel, your father.}

From Asher
shall come the richest food
and he will provide
the king's delicacies.

Naphtali
is a deer let loose.
He delivers
words
of beauty."

Vayechi 49:20-21

Q. What do "words of beauty" mean to you? How careful are you with your words?

{Jacob is dying and is surrounded by his twelve sons. He tells them what will befall them in the end of days. He said, "Listen to Israel, your father.}

Son of grace is Joseph.
A son of grace to the eyes
and the women gazed.
There were those
who heaped bitter abuse upon him and
making him their target. How the arrow-
tongued men hated him!

But he kept serenely resolute
and his arms {eventually} became bedecked with gold
from the hands of the mighty Power of Jacob.
From there he shepherded the rock of Israel.
{All of this} from God of your father Who will
continue to help you. You will remain with God
All-Sufficing Who will continue to bless you
{with}
blessings of heaven from above
blessings of the depths below and
blessings of the breast and womb.
May the blessings of your father add to those
of my parents to the endless bounds of the
hills eternal. Let them be upon the head of
Joseph and
upon the head of the one separated from his brothers."

Vayechi 49:22-26

Q. What is grace? How can you remain positive amidst negative people?

{Jacob is dying and is surrounded by his twelve sons. He tells them what will befall them in the end of days. He said, "Listen to Israel, your father.}

Benjamin
will tear the wolf to pieces.
He will devour his prey in the morning
and in the evening he will distribute {the} spoils."

{In total} these are the tribes of Israel.
Twelve in all.

This is what their father said to them when he blessed them. He blessed each of {his sons} according to his appropriate blessing.

Vayechi 49:27-28

Q. What makes blessings appropriate? When do you feel blessed?

{After giving each of his sons blessings}
Jacob said to them
"I shall be gathered to my peoples.
Bury me with my fathers in the cave
in the field of Machpelah
on the land Abraham bought.
There
they buried Abraham and his wife Sarah.
Isaac and his wife Rebecca {and}
where I buried Leah.
The field and cave were bought from sons of Heth."

When Jacob finished, he drew his feet into
the bed and died and was gathered to his
people.
And Joseph fell upon his father
and wept over him and kissed him.

He ordered his servants to have him embalmed so he could
fulfill his promise to bury him in Canaan.

Vayechi 49:29-50:2

Q. What makes a burial site sacred? What does it mean to be gathered
to your people?

{Overseer Joseph ordered his father Jacob embalmed.}

It took forty days for embalming
and thus Egypt mourned {Jacob} for seventy days.

When the period of mourning was over
Joseph went to Pharaoh "My father bound
me by an oath {to bury him with his fathers
in the Cave of Machpelah.}
Now, if you allow me, I will go north and bury my father. I will
return."

Pharaoh said, "Go bury your father
just as he had you promise."

Vayechi 50:3-6

Q. To what oaths are you bound? How do you mourn?

Joseph headed north to bury his father
along with Pharaoh's courtiers, Egypt's elders
all his household and his brothers' and father's family. Only
the young children and flocks remained in Egypt when
Overseer Joseph and his grand procession of chariots {went
to bury his father Jacob (Israel).}

They came to Goren HaAtad
which is across the Jordan river on the bank
and there they held
a very great and impressive eulogy.

And Joseph ordained
a seven-day mourning period for his father.

When the Canaanite inhabitants saw this mourning they said,
"This is a grievous mourning for Egypt." Therefore
they named this river bank, "Egypt's Mourning".

{Jacob's} sons did for him exactly as
he instructed them. His sons carried
him to Canaan and buried him in the
purchased land in the Cave of Machpelah.

Vayechi 50:7-13

Q. What is the value of having set times for mourning? How do you
want to be eulogized?

After he buried his father
Joseph {Egypt's Overseer of grain}
returned to Egypt with his brothers
and all the others who had come to bury his father.

Joseph's brothers saw that their father was dead and they
said {to each other} "Perhaps Joseph holds a silent grudge
against us. Surely he will repay us all
for the evil we did him."

Vayechi 50:14-15

Q. How does death affect relationships? What purpose do grudges
serve?

{After their father died the brothers said
"Surely Joseph will repay us all
for the evil we did to him."}

So they went to the Overseer's household supervisor and
instructed him to say
to their brother Joseph, "Your father
gave orders before his death.
He said, 'You shall say to Joseph
"O please
kindly forgive
the spiteful deeds
of the servants of your father's God'."

And Joseph wept when they spoke to him.

His brothers themselves also went and flung themselves
before him and said, "We are ready to be your slaves."

Vayechi 50:16-18

Q. How do you ask forgiveness? What does forgiving do for you?

{Fearing retaliation from Joseph as Egypt's Overseer, the
brothers flung themselves before their brother
and said, "We are ready to be your slaves."}

But Joseph said, "Fear not for am I in the place of God? Even
though you intended harm God intended it for good. It is as
clear as the day
that God accomplished a way of keeping our vast people
alive. So fear not
I will sustain you and your little ones."

And thus
Joseph comforted them
by speaking to their hearts.

Vayechi 50:19-21

Q. How do you speak to someone's heart? What have you
accomplished?

Tiptoe Through Genesis

Joseph dwelt in Egypt he and his father's household and lived
until he was 110 years old.
Joseph {who had become Viceroy of
Egypt} saw three generations of his
sons. He said to his brothers
"I am about to die but
God will surely remember you and bring you out of this land
to the land
God swore to Abraham, Isaac and Jacob."

Then
Joseph made the Children of Israel
swear "When God will indeed
remember you then
you must bring my bones with you
up and out of here."

Joseph died at the age of hundred and ten years and they
embalmed him and he was placed in a sarcophagus in Egypt.

Vayechi 50: 22-26

Q. When it comes to being buried, what's important to you? When have
you been the holder of valuables?